50

1968-2018

The Sydney Taylor Book Award

A Guide to the Winners, Honor Books and Notables

Edited by Chava Pinchuck

Association of Jewish Libraries

BSD

Compiled and edited by Chava Pinchuck.

With thanks to Kathleen Bloomfield, Rachel Kamin, Susan Kusel and Laura Schutzman.

Cover Design by Jonathan Fields

ISBN: 978-0-929262-05-5

www.jewishlibraries.org

The Association of Jewish Libraries promotes Jewish literacy through enhancement of library and library resources and through leadership for the profession and practitioners of Judaica librarianship.

Interview and photographs of Richard Michelson and Karla Gudeon are courtesy of Barbara Bietz from her Jewish Books for Kids blog post of February 4, 2018, part of the Sydney Taylor Book Award Blog Tour: http://jewishbooksforkids.com/2018/02/04/sydney-taylor-book-award-blog-tour-the-language-of-angels-a-story-about-the-reinvention-of-hebrew/. Accessed on April 25, 2018 and used with permission.

On the auspicious occasion of the 50th Anniversary of the Sydney Taylor Book Award I would like to thank the Association of Jewish Libraries and all the members of the Sydney Taylor Award Committees who have helped make my mother's books into enduring children's classics.

It's no surprise that the wonderful "Library Lady" had such a central role in the *All-of-a-Kind Family* stories. Little Sarah (aka Sydney) would have been so happy that her penny-a-day late book return fee would mean so much and someday become so famous.

My congratulations and best wishes to all the Jewish library ladies and gentlemen for at least another 50 years, lots more award-winning authors, and happy reading!

Jo Taylor Marshall
Daughter of Sydney Taylor

Table of Contents

The Sydney Taylor Book Award

Association of Jewish Libraries

Mission

The purpose of the Sydney Taylor Book Award is to encourage the publication of outstanding books of Jewish content for children, books that exemplify the highest literary standards while authentically portraying the Jewish experience. We hope that official recognition of such books will inspire authors, encourage publishers, inform parents and teachers, and intrigue young readers. We also hope that by educating readers about the Jewish experience, we can engender pride in Jewish readers while building bridges to readers of other backgrounds.

History

The Association of Jewish Libraries (AJL) has been recognizing quality Jewish literature for many years. In 1968, AJL established a children's book award called the Shirley Kravitz Children's Book Award. The first winner of this award was author Esther Hautzig for her book *The Endless Steppe* (HarperCollins, 1968). This award was renamed "the Sydney Taylor Book Award" in 1978 after the death of Sydney Taylor, author of the *All-of-a-Kind Family* series.

Nettie Frishman, a librarian Los Angeles Public Library and a member of the AJL book award committee, was a friend of Ralph and Sydney Taylor, and created a "shidduch" between Ralph and AJL. Ralph established the Sydney Taylor Book Award in his wife's memory. The first winner under the award's new name was Doris Orgel for *The Devil in Vienna* (Penguin, 1978). Ralph Taylor attended the June 1979 AJL convention for the awards ceremony. He was presented with the Sydney Taylor Body-of-Work Award as a posthumous prize for his wife's writing career, in which he had been very instrumental.

Since the re-naming of the award, all winners of AJL's children's book awards have generally been referred to as winners of the Sydney Taylor Book Award.

From 1968 to 1980, AJL selected a single award winner from among the novels and chapter books published each year for older children. In 1981, the Sydney Taylor Book Award began recognizing winners in two categories: a picture book or short informational book in the Younger Readers Category and a novel or longer nonfiction title in the Older Readers Category.

In 1985, the Sydney Taylor Book Award Committee began designating Notable Books (originally called "The Best of the Bunch"). These are books which have not been selected as prize winners, but are deemed worthy of attention. A new list of Notable Books is publicized each year at the same time that the winners are announced. Notable Books are selected in both the Younger and Older Readers Categories.

In 1988, the Sydney Taylor Book Award Committee began selecting Honor Books as well as winning titles. The Honor Books bear a silver seal, while the winning titles bear a gold seal. Honor Books are now selected in all three categories: for Younger Readers, for Older Readers, and for Teen Readers.

From 1968 to 2004, the awards were named for the year in which the winners were published, not the year in which the award was presented. For example, the 2004 Sydney Taylor Book Award winner, *Real Time* by Pnina Moed Kass, was published in 2004, yet the prize was awarded in 2005. In 2005, the dating system was changed to coordinate with that used by other major children's book awards such as ALA's Newbery and Caldecott Awards. From that time forth, the award was named for the year in which the prize was presented, for a book published during the previous year.

Over the years, the Sydney Taylor Book Award Committee received an increasing number of young adult titles, geared for 7th - 12th grade, giving the "Older Readers" category too wide of an age range to evaluate properly. With approval from the AJL Board and Council, the Committee established the Association of Jewish Libraries Teen Book Award in January 2007 to recognize the best books of Jewish content for teen readers. In March 2007, the family of Sydney Taylor generously offered to fund the new category. The Sydney Taylor Book Awards are now presented in three categories: Younger Readers, Older Readers, and Teen Readers.

Criteria and Scoring

Criteria

The criteria used to evaluate books for the Sydney Taylor Book Award are:

The book has literary merit.

The book has positive, or at least authentic, Jewish religious or cultural content. "Positive" is sometimes problematic, as in books which depict self-image problems of Jewish characters during the Holocaust, so this is a grey area.

The book is appropriate for the intended grade level in style, vocabulary, format, and illustration.

Whether fiction or nonfiction, the book is solidly rooted in authentic and accurate detail, through scholarship and research by the author.

Textbooks and reprints are not eligible, although revised editions and re-illustrated editions are eligible. Liturgical books (prayer books) are not eligible.

Try to remember to judge the books not only within the pool of STBA submissions, but to compare them to truly excellent literature such as your favorite Caldecott and Newbery winners. Inconsistent quality is an ongoing issue within Jewish children's publishing. There are some very earnest but not very well produced books published each year within our genre. Because of this, the smaller number of better-quality books we receive may take on a glow of excellence that is not realistic. Be sure to keep your perspective on the quality of the books under consideration.

Please evaluate the books using the criteria listed above, as well as looking at overall quality. Books lacking Jewish content are not eligible, but remember that quality is more important than quantity — sometimes a well-done book containing only a minor amount of Jewish content may indeed be eligible.

Scoring Books

Provide a rating for each book:

N/A = not eligible (due to no Jewish content, wrong publication year, not juvenile literature, reprint, textbook, etc.)
0 = Objectionable (inaccurate, biased, etc.)
1 = Poor
2 = Average
3 = Good (Notable Book contender)
4 = Great (Honor Book contender)
5 = Excellent (Award contender)

In other words, scoring a book a 3 means that you are recommending it for our Notable List; scoring a book a 4 means you think it should be considered for the Honor Award (silver medal); and scoring a book a 5 means you think it should be considered for the Award (gold medal). So as odd as it seems, 2 isn't really a bad score – think of it as a book that most libraries would still want to purchase if there's a need, but that does not belong on the Notable List.

Please give each book a single rating – do not give separate ratings, for instance, for style and content.

Try to stick to whole numbers, but you may add a .5 to a score when necessary.

Because we do not see all the books at once, scoring can be difficult because we don't know what we will be comparing to. You will have the opportunity to adjust your scores at the end of the year.

Things to think about:

Consider plot development, character development, language and writing style, setting, point of view or bias of the author, and theme.

When appropriate, compare with other titles treating similar themes or subjects, or other titles by the same author.

Think about the usability of the book for librarians, teachers, and families. When possible, try out the books on real, live children to get their reactions and opinions.

Comment on sloppy or incorrect text or illustrations. Point out terminology that reveals a Christian point of view such as "Old Testament," "B.C." or "A.D.," and Jesus "Christ." Point out skewed theological interpretations and Christian biblical perspectives. Watch out for words or illustrations that denigrate Jewish or other cultures.

Remember that the illustrations are as important as the text. Evaluate the quality, effectiveness, and clarity of the illustrations. Do the illustrations reinforce the mood or action of the text? This is particularly important for picture books, but it also applies to any book that contains illustrations, photographs, maps, etc. Also think about the appropriateness of page layout and design.

Consider whether the index, glossary, etc. are excellent, incomplete, inaccurate, etc.

The committee members report their scoring to the chair. Deliberations take place in late December and early January of each year.

Who Was Sydney Taylor?

By June Cummins, a"h

The Family

At the turn of the last century, the Brenner family emigrated to the United States, as so many Jewish families did. Four years after they arrived, their third daughter, Sarah Brenner, was born on October 30, 2004. Later, Sarah changed her name to Sydney, but her four sisters, Ella, Henrietta, Charlotte and Gertrude, kept their first names, and Sydney immortalized these names by giving them to their character counterparts in her *All-of-a-Kind Family* books. Three brothers were subsequently born. Jerry, the youngest brother, died on August 5, 2010.

As a grown woman, Sydney remembered the early days of her family's life on the Lower East Side. Although they were poor, like most Jewish immigrants, they had many happy times. Just like the girls in the books, Sydney and her sisters were "five little girls [who] shared one bedroom -- and never minded bedtime. Snuggled in our beds we would talk and giggle and plan tomorrow's fun and mischief." (*Something about the Author*)

The Story

When Sydney had her own child, Jo, she told her stories of her childhood on the Lower East Side. Sydney felt Jo was lonely as an only child and wanted to share her past with her. "When Jo was little...I would sit beside her bed at night and try to make up for the lack of a big family by telling her about my own. Jo loved the stories about how Papa and Mama worked and how the five little girls helped out. She was delighted with the tales of our good times together and the enjoyment of simple pleasures. She loved the stories so much that I decided to write them all down especially for her. The manuscript went into a big box and stayed there." (*More Books by More People*)

The Book

One summer when Sydney was away working as the drama counselor at Camp CEJWIN, her husband Ralph decided to submit the manuscript to a contest sponsored by Follett. Sydney has no idea of his action until she received a letter in the mail. "No one was more surprised than I when I received a letter from Mrs. Meeks, the Children's Book Editor of Wilcox & Follett, telling me she wanted to publish *All-of-a-Kind-Family*. I didn't know what she was talking about. I told my husband and the whole story came out. Then Mr. Follett telephoned me to say that *All-of-a-Kind-Family* had won the Follett [Award]." (*Something about the Author*)

The Series

After the success of the first *All-of-a-Kind-Family* book, Sydney went on to write four more for the series (*More All-of-a-Kind-Family*, *All-of-a-Kind-Family Uptown*, *All-of-a-Kind-Family Downtown*, and *Ella of All-of-a-Kind-Family*), as well as several other books for children. She toured schools and libraries all over the country, talking to children about her work. She also continued to work at Camp Cejwin and was there for over thirty years.

The Legacy

Sydney died of cancer on February 12, 1978. Although some of her books are over fifty years old, they are still beloved by many -- both old and young (and in between) -- today. *The All-of-a-Kind-Family* books have been reissued several times, most recently in 2014 by Lizzie Skurnick Books. The Museum at Eldridge Street on the Lower East Side of New York City offers an "All-of-a-Kind Family Walking Tour" where participants "stroll through the story and onto the streets as they buy pickles, stop at a candy store, and bring Sydney Taylor's beloved novel to life." Linking up her past with her daughter's present, Sydney made the Lower East Side of the early twentieth century come vividly alive for thousands of readers.

NOTE:
The original article was written for the AJL *All-of-a-Kind-Family Companion* (available at www.jewishlibraries.org). In 2004 by June Cummins, who was an Associate Professor in the Department of English and Comparative Literature at San Diego State University. June died in February 2018, and this updated version is included as a both professional and personal tribute to her scholarship and friendship. Her biography of Sydney Taylor will be published posthumously.

The Language of Angels: A Story about the Reinvention of Hebrew

Past Chair Barbara Bietz talks with author Richard Michelson and illustrator Karla Gudeon, winner of the 2018 Sydney Taylor Book Award for Younger Readers

Rich, you provide some fascinating details in the telling of Eliezer's quest to create Modern Hebrew. What sparked your interest in Eliezer and how extensive was your research?

In 2001, while collaborating on *Too Young for Yiddish* (Charlesbridge, 2002 -- a 2002 Notable Book for Older Readers), illustrator Neil Waldman and I were discussing Isaac Bashevis Singer's claim that Yiddish was the only language without a word for "armaments." I asked Neil his thoughts about whether the culture informs the language or the language informs the culture. I don't recall our conclusions, but during that lunch, Neil mentioned Eliezer Ben Yehuda and his quest to make Hebrew the daily language of the Jews. I was fascinated. I had never heard the story, and to me, Ben-Yehuda was no more than a street name in Israel. How do you reinvent a language that died out in daily use almost two millennia ago? How do you make up names for everything new that came along in 2000 years– ice cream, bicycles, libraries? Imagine going to Italy today and convincing everyone to speak Latin – and succeeding within a couple of generations! I love words, and as a child, I thought Adam must have had great fun naming all of the animals. It never occurred to me how much work that would entail.

Neil said: "I was going to write Ben-Yehuda's story, but couldn't find my way in. I now give you the idea as a gift." I read everything I could on the subject (my bibliography is listed in the back of my book) but abandoned the project – also unable to find a way to make the story accessible for kids. More than fifteen years later, researching my book *Fascinating: The Life of Leonard Nimoy* (Knopf Books for Young Readers 2016 -- a 2017 Sydney Taylor Honor Book), I went to a Star Trek Convention where a father had his son speak to me in Klingon. How crazy is that! The kid was four or five and didn't speak English. What kind of meshugganah father teaches his kid to speak Klingon instead of English? Then I remembered Ben-Yehuda. I'd found my way into the story.

Karla, your art is such a lovely accompaniment to the rich text of the story. What was your first response when you read the manuscript? How much research did you need to do to create the art?

My first thought was "I'm so honored that Rich hand-picked me for this project and what a terrific opportunity this is to work with my phenomenally talented, funny, & yes, incredibly handsome friend Rich Michelson." I feel Rich could make a fascinating book out of any topic, but one that deals with Hebrew and etymology was of particular interest to me. Growing up, if I was to feel an integral part of family gatherings, I needed to become a wicked good scrabble player. Words were everything. My grandmother was notorious for knowing obscure, wonderful "scrabble words" so much so, that we would hesitate to challenge her when we weren't sure if a word was real or invented by her. Part of the "fun" was finding out at the end of the game, which words were real and which were bluffs. We had to become experts at discerning why a word might be a word. I love combining text and clever titles with my art, the act of illustrating, and now illustrating a text ABOUT text was a dream come true.

As far as research goes for the artwork, I relied on tried and true methods, books, questioning, and the almighty Google Images. Rich provided me with some valuable background material, I found some source images on my own through books and photographic imagery. I asked my favorite Hebrew experts, my step-father Marvin Antosofsky, a learned Rabbi and Cantor, and childhood Jewish sleep-away camp friend, Cindy, a superintendent of Jewish Day Schools, for any background info they might have that could inform my pictures.

I loved learning about Eliezer Ben-Yehuda and his relationship with Ben-Zion. Like Rich, I am not fully comfortable with the way Eliezer used his own child to further his personal goal. However, I did find I found joy in thinking about the excitement of creating and forging the Hebrew language together as a family unit. The younger of my two grown sons, Max (21), often takes an oppositional viewpoint to my own, when discussing politics and world events. He likes to remind me how important it is for him to form his own opinions. He claims I tried to force him to lean very, very, very far to the left. While he is a predominantly liberal thinker, he says that he would have liked to have had more opportunities to come to his own conclusions. Rather than the example he gives of growing up with a mom that prompted him at eight years old to answer the question "Do you think there is there anything you can do that your mom wouldn't forgive you for?" with the answer, "Yes, marry a social conservative." My point is, I think all parents at some point force their own agenda on their children. Eliezer Ben-Yehuda just did that to a different degree.

Rich, Eliezer's son, Ben-Zion is isolated from other kids because of his father's insistence that he only speak Hebrew. Although Eliezer's plan ultimately found success it seems Ben-Zion paid a price. What are your thoughts about Ben-Zion's sacrifice?

Had I lived at the time, I'd have certainly joined the rest of the neighborhood in considering Ben Yehuda a child abuser. He put his dream of a common language for Jews ahead of his family's well-being. Does one need that kind of drive to succeed as he did? It is one thing to sacrifice your own life, but to experiment with your child! He wanted his son to be the first native Hebrew speaker in modern times—and he would not allow him to hear any other spoken language (he even covered Ben-Zion's ears when animals were nearby). I'd have had a difficult time finding any sympathy for Ben Yehuda and writing this story if not for Ben-Zion's own later writings, which emphasized his love of his father. Ben-Zion became a man of words himself -an author and a journalist–and furthered his father's vision. He renamed himself Itamar Ben-Avi—Son of my Father.

Karla, can you tell me a bit about your artistic process, what medium you used, etc? Were you able to collaborate with Rich at all during the process?

My artistic process for illustrating a book is both solitary and social. I like doing all the initial brainstorming by myself. I say brainstorming rather than sketching, because I like thinking and mapping the book out in words and concepts before even sketching. In this initial phase, I'll list and describe my ideas for what I think compliments the language page by page.

With book illustration, the illustrator isn't always able to consult with the author. Working with Rich directly for years and knowing him so well gave me the invaluable ability to call and e-mail and refine my concepts to better suit the text.

My illustrating process has changed a great deal over the years. Where I used to sketch, re-sketch, erase, start again, trace, back-trace etc. I now start with a combination of sketching and making compositional collages.I combine my own characters and designs with imagery I cull and put the composition together in photoshop so I can "see" the overall composition and elements of the piece along with the text. Once I'm satisfied with the composition I then print the page and rework the piece with #2 pencil "Karla-fying" the entire image.

 I am incredibly fortunate to have fabulously friends, relatives, and a studio team that I can rely on to give honest critiques and feedback through all the stages of my process
Often, I'll redraw parts after my brother Adam Gudeon, an artist/author/illustrator and a studio team provide their critique and we discuss the pieces. Once the final drawing is set, I ink the line work and work out a general color palette for the book which I execute with watercolors.

Rich and Karla, what is the most interesting or unexpected thing you have learned in the process of creating and publishing The Language of Angels?

Rich: The story itself is so interesting and amazing that everything blew me away. But I was very surprised to learn that, while most Jews living in Jerusalem at the time shunned Ben-Yehuda, he found common cause with many of the native Arabs living in what was then called Palestine. Ben-Yehuda delivered a lecture at the Arabic Academy of Science and told his audience about the close relationship between Arabic and Hebrew. He explained how he had borrowed many words from Arabic and that some Arabic words had been borrowed from Hebrew. Most Arabs respected Eliezer and were pleased to hear their "sister tongue" spoken in the markets. Ben-Yehuda believed that Jews and Arabs were mishpacha— family—and should share the land and live together.

And here is a side tidbit which occurs after the book's timeframe. Just as Ben-Yehuda wanted all Jews to speak a common language, Ben-Zion wanted all people to communicate directly, and so championed Esperanto. In 1966 Hollywood produced *Incubis*, a (terrible) feature filmed entirely in Esperanto. It starred a pre-trek William Shatner.

Karla: I was surprised to learn that there was a sizable portion of the population not only at the time that objected to Hebrew becoming the language franca, but that there are still people that feel this way. That Hebrew is the holy tongue and shouldn't be used for the mundane; it should be spoken and written only for prayer. Prior to *The Language of Angels*, I hadn't made the connection that this is why some Hasidic sects speak only Yiddish, not Hebrew. *Meshugge*, right?!?!

Thank you, Richard and Karla! Congratulations to you both!

Sydney Taylor Book Award Winners, Honor Books and Notables

2018 Awards

Younger Readers
The Language of Angels: A Story about the Reinvention of Hebrew
by Richard Michelson.
Illustrations by Karla Gudeon.
Charlesbridge
ISBN: 978-1580896368

This beautiful picture book tells the story of how Hebrew became an everday language in Israel, after being out of use for two thousand years. The folk art illustrations are an illuminating match.

Older Readers

Refugee by Alan Gratz.
Scholastic
ISBN: 9780545880831

The journeys of three different young refugees from Nazi Germany, 1990s Cuba and present day Syria come together to form an emotional and timely narrative about the refugee experience.

Teen Readers

The Librarian of Auschwitz by Antonio Iturbe.
Translated by Lilit Thwaites
Godwin Books, an imprint of Henry Holt and Company
ISBN: 9781627796187

This powerful story of Dita Kraus and her protection of a handful of books in the Auschwitz concentration camp shows the importance of hope in the darkest of times.

Honor Books
Younger Readers

Yaffa and Fatima: Shalom, Salaam adapted by Fawzia Gilani-Williams.
Illustrations by Chiara Fedele.
Kar-Ben Publishing
ISBN: 9781467789387

Jewish Yaffa and Arab Fatima are neighbors whose concern for each other during a date shortage provides a new twist on the "Brothers" legend. Burgundy and teal against neutral backgrounds provide striking illustrations for a story with a subtle, yet timely message.

Drop by Drop: A Story of Rabbi Akiva by Jacqueline Jules.
Illustrated by Yevgenia Nayberg.
Kar-Ben Publishing
ISBN: 9781512420906

Skeptical that he can start learning Torah at the age of forty, when illiterate shepherd Akiva sees the way water has worn down the rocks in the brook, he applies himself and becomes the great Rabbi Akiva, thanks in great part to his wife Rachel's devotion and trust. Colorful and folksy illustrations complement the text.

Older Readers

Viva Rose! by Susan Krawitz.
Holiday House
ISBN: 9780823437566

Rose's brother Abraham joins Pancho Villa's army. When trying to get a letter to him, Rose is kidnapped and becomes the playmate of Dorotea. First-person narrative and historic details of the late 19th century Mexcian revolutionary enhance the story.

This Is Just a Test by Madelyn Rosenberg and Wendy Wan-Long Shang.
Scholastic
ISBN: 9781338037722

David Da-Wei Horowitz is preparing for his bar mitzvah, and trying to appease both his Jewish and Chinese grandmothers, and digging a fallout shelter, and trying to balance his friends. Add a little 1980s David Hasselhoff and Betamax for a quirky and fast-paced read.

The Six-Day Hero by Tammar Stein.
Kar-Ben Publishing
ISBN: 9781512458718

Stein has penned an "intense read about family, love, identity and spirituality" that takes place on the eve of Israel's Six-Day War in 1967, with twelve-year-old Motti both idolizing and resenting his older brother Gideon, who will be a soldier in the war.

Teen Readers

To Look a Nazi in the Eye: A Teen's Account of a War Criminal Trial by **Kathy Kacer with Jordana Lebowitz.**
Second Story Press
ISBN: 9781772600407

Lebowitz attended the first week of the trial of Oskar Groening, known as "the bookkeeper of Auschwitz." She blogged about her experience, and as the granddaughter of Holocaust survivors, went through a myriad of emotions. Kacer chronicles both her account and the trial testimony. She returned to Canada and closely followed the rest of the trial (Groening was found guilty of facilitating mass murder and sentenced to four years in prison, but he died before he began his sentence). Lebowitz is now a human rights advocate.

Almost Autumn by **Marianne Kaurin.**
Translated by Rosie Hedger.
Arthur A. Levine Books, an imprint of Scholastic
ISBN: 9780545889650

Ilse Stern is stood up for what was to be her first date with her crush and neighbor Hermann Rod, and things get more complicated from there. Hermann joins the resistance and Ilse's family faces the anti-Semitism of Quisling's Norway during World War II. Will first love triumph?

The Girl with the Red Balloon (The Balloonmakers) by **Katherine Locke.**
Albert Whitlman
ISBN: 9780807529379

Time travel and a red balloon propel Ellie Baum to 1988 East Berlin, where she must fight the evils of dark magic that are trying to change history.

Notable Books

Younger Readers

Yom Kippur Shortstop by David A. Adler.
Illustrations by Andre Ceolin.
Apples & Honey Press, an imprint of Behrman House
ISBN: 9781681155210

Inspired by Sandy Koufax's legendary dilemma, Jacob must decide whether to play the championship Little League game, or sit it out on the holiest day in the Jewish calendar.

Under the Sabbath Lamp by Michael Herman.
Illustrations by Alida Massari
Kar-Ben Publishing
ISBN: 9781512408416

Instead of Sabbath candles, Izzy and Olivia Bloom have a interesting Sabbath lamp that burns olive oil. Their neighbors learn that its history is also interesting, traveling from the *shtetl* to America one piece at a time with each family member that immigrated.

Big Sam: A Rosh Hashanah Tall Tale by Eric A. Kimmel.
Illustrations by Jim Starr.
Apples & Honey Press, an imprint of Behrman House
ISBN: 9781681155258

How big is Big Sam? So big that in order to make his challahs for the New Year, he digs out the Grand Canyon for a mixing bowl and bakes it in Mount St. Helens. Then, it being the time of year for repentance, he cleans up the mess he made in his preparation and shares his Rosh Hashanah foods with friends. Beautiful illustrations of the American West amplify the text.

The Knish War on Rivington Street by Joanne Oppenheim.
Illustrations by Jon Davis.
Albert Whitman
ISBN: 9780807541821

Square or round? A price war ensues, but either way, everyone loves knishes, so there will be plenty of business for both Benny's family store and the Tisch's new store across the street.

Ruth Bader Ginsburg: The Case of R.B.G. vs. Inequality by Jonah Winter.
Illustrations by Stacy Innerst.
Abraims Books for Young Readers
ISBN: 9781419725593

How many injustices did Ruth Bader Ginsburg suffer before becoming a Supreme Court Justice (and a hipster idol)? The case presented to the reader includes the biases against Jews, women, and working mothers in both academia and the work world. The goache, ink and Photostop illustrations add humor, while the author's note supplies the details of the discrimation Ginsberg faced throughout her career.

Older Readers

Hedy's Journey: The True Story of a Hungarian Girl Fleeing the Holocaust **(Encounter: Narrative Nonfiction Picture Books) by Michelle Bisson. Illustrations by El primo Ramón.**
Capstone Press
ISBN: 9781515782223
Hedy leaves Hungary in 1941, and she must way her way to America alone. Her journey is frught with both fortune and misfortune, and both happiness and sadness. Based on the author's mother's experiences.

The Children of Willesden Lane: A True Story of Hope and Survival during Wold War II: Young Readers Edition **by Mona Golabek and Lee Cohen and adapted by Emil Sher.**
Little Brown Books for Young Readers, a division of Hachette Book Group
ISBN: 9780316554886

Adapted from the original (Grand Central Publishing, 2003), Golabek's mother's leaves her idyllic life in Vienna, and travels on the *Kindertransport* to her new home in an orphanage outside London. Worried about family and old friends, her new friends bolster her as she fulfills her potential as a musical prodigy and eventually attends the Royal Academy of Music on a scholarship.

Wordwings **by Sydelle Pearl.**
Guernica Editions
ISBN: 9781771831963

Emanuel Ringelblum organized an archive and collected diaries and documents to chronicle life in the Warsaw Ghetto. Twelve-year-old Rivka Rosenfeld writes her thoughts between the pages of a Hans Christian Andersen book, which is also hidden in a milkcan for posterity.

The Dollmaker of Krakow by **R. M. Romero.**
Delcorte Press, an imprint of Random House Children's Books
ISBN: 9781524715397

Fairy tale and harsh reality intertwine as Karolina the doll, is brought by a "kind wind" to the shop of Cyryl the dollmaker. They try to help violinist Josef and his daughter Rena escape the Krakow ghetto and avoid extermination by the Nazis.

Teen Readers

Man's Search for Meaning: Young Reader Edition by **Viktor E. Frankl.**
Beacon Press
ISBN: 9780807067994

Frankl's best selling work has been abridged, with much of the discussion of scientific and philosophical references left out and more focus on the meaning of life and the meaning of suffering John Boyne (*Boy in the Striped Pyjamas* (David Fickling Books, 2006)), wrote the Foreword which describes his introduction to Frankl's book and its "profound effect" on him.

Ronit & Jamil by **Pamela L. Laskin.**
Katherine Tegen Books, an imprint of HarperCollins
ISBN: 9780062458544

Much like Romeo and Juliet, Israeli Ronit and Palestinian Jamil are star-crossed lovers whose families are against their relationship. Their story is told with quotes from Shakespeare and Arab poets and use of the ghazal (the rhyme is repeated in the even lines) form of poetry.

Stolen Secrets by **L. B. Schulman.**
Boyds Mills Press, a division of Highlights
ISBN: 9781629797229

Livvy's grandmother Adelle, whom Livvy had thought was dead, suffers from Alzheimer's Disease. As Livvy gets to know her grandmother and reads her journal entries, she learns that Adelle was in a concentration camp and may have a connection to Anne Frank. Things go awry when Livvy's mother ends up back in rehab, and Livvy and friend Franklin D. must protect Adelle.

2017 Awards

Younger Readers

I Dissent: Ruth Bader Ginsburg Makes Her Mark by Debbie Levy.
Illustrations by Elizabeth Baddeley.
Simon & Schuster Books for Young Readers
ISBN: 9781481465595

This delightful biography of the Supreme Court Justice teaches children that dissent does not make a person disagreeable, and can even help change the world. The grab-your-attention illustrations help explain the text.

Older Readers

The Inquisitor's Tale: Or, The Three Magical Children and Their Holy Dog
by Adam Gidwitz.
Illustrations by Hatem Aly.
Dutton Children's Books, an imprint of Penguin Random House
ISBN: 97805254261

Part fantasy and part adventure, this is the tale of strangers who become friends while on a quest to save thousands of volumes of Talmud. The beautiful illuminations reflect the medieval flavor of the book.

Teen Readers

Anna and the Swallow Man by Gavriel Savit.
Alfred A. Knopf, an imprint of Penguin Random House
ISBN: 9780553513349

Anna is left alone in 1939 Krakow when the Nazis take her father away. She meets the mysterious Swallow Man who is able to speak "bird," and travels with him in the forests of Poland, where they spend four years hiding and eluding capture. This is a haunting story that may be allegory or folktaleor perhaps both.

Honor Books

Younger Readers

A Hat for Mrs. Goldman: A Story about Knitting and Love by Michelle Edwards.
Illustrations by G. Brian Karas.
Schwartz and Wade Books, an imprint of Penguin Random House
ISBN: 9780553497106
Kind Mrs. Goldman, assisted by her young next-door neighbor Sophia, knits hats for everyone in their neighborhood. But who will knit a hat for Mrs. Goldman? Sophia tries, and the result is much appreciated (if not perfectly executed). A warm intergenerational and intercultural friendship story.

Fascinating: The Life of Leonard Nimoy by Richard Michelson.
Illustrations by Edel Rodriguez.
Alfred A. Knopf, an imprint of Penguin Random House
ISBN: 9781101933305

Michelson, longtime friend and gallerist for the Star Trek actor and photographer, presents a personal and heartfelt picture-book biography of the late Leonard Nimoy, from Nimoy's observant Jewish upbringing to his childhood interest in photography to his iconic television role. Groovy, out-of-this-world illustrations reflect the time period.

Older Readers

Dreidels on the Brain by Joel Ben Izzy.
Dial Books for Young Readers, an imprint of Penguin Random House
ISBN: 9780803740976

In this semi-autobiographical story set during Hanukkah 1971, twelve-year-old Joel describes his family and life in the L.A. suburbs. His observations are frequently hilarious, even as his family faces serious events (his father spends much of that week in the hospital).

A Poem for Peter: The Story of Ezra Jack Keats and the Creation of The Snowy Day by Andrea Davis Pinkney.
Illustrations by Steve Johnson and Lou Fancher.
Viking Children's Books, an imprint of Penguin Random House
ISBN: 9780425287682

This gorgeously illustrated ode to the author of the iconic picture book *The Snowy Day* focuses on Keats's background as a child of Polish immigrants, his early artwork, and his attention to discrimination and social justice. The lyrical text is addressed to Peter, Keats's most well-known and beloved character.

Teen Readers

No Honor Books recognized.

Notable Books

Younger Readers

The Sundown Kid: A Southwestern Shabbat **by Barbara Bietz.**
Illustrations by John Kanzler.
August House Publishing
ISBN: 9781939160942

In this unique Southwestern-set frontier tale, the young narrator's family introduces Shabbat foods and customs to its new community, making someplace far away from extended family feel more like home. An author's note tells more about Jews in the "Wild West" and about *hachnasat orchim* ("the act of welcoming guests").

On One Foot **by Linda Glaser.**
Illustrations by Nuria Balaguer.
Kar-Ben Publishing
ISBN: 9781467778428

A young Torah scholar asks: "Can you teach me the whole Torah while standing on one foot?" He's repeatedly rebuffed ("That's preposterous!" "Ha! Not even the great Rabbi Hillel can do that!"), before finally meeting that learned man himself and fulfilling his quest. Mixed-media illustrations cleverly incorporate papers with Hebrew writing.

The Tree in the Courtyard: Looking through Anne Frank's Window **by Jeff Gottesfeld.**
Illustrations by Peter McCarty.
Alfred A. Knopf, an imprint of Random House
ISBN: 9780385753975

Lyrical text and dramatic brown-ink illustrations on creamy paper depict the story of the Frank family from the third-person perspective of the tree that stood outside Anne's window of the attic annex. An afterword tells more: "Saplings and seedpods from Anne Frank's tree have been planted around the world."

***Gabriel's Horn* by Eric Kimmel.**
Illustrations by Maria Surducan.
Kar-Ben Publishing
ISBN: 9781467789363

On Erev Rosh Hashanah, a soldier knocks on Gabriel's family's door, owners of an antique shop. About to deploy, the soldier entrusts his French horn to them. Good fortune follows the family as they perform other good deeds, shown in luminous illustrations.

***Chicken Soup, Chicken Soup* by Pamela Mayer.**
Illustrations by Deborah Melmon.
Kar-Ben Publishing
ISBN: 9781467789349

"Two grandmas, Two soup pots, and Two family traditions" lead to "the first ever Jewish Chinese Kreplach Wonton Chicken Soup!" prepared by young Sophie, which pleases both her bubbe and her nai nai (Chinese for grandmother).

***Not This Turkey!* By Jessica Steinberg.**
Illustrations by Amanda Pike.
Albert Whitman & Company
ISBN: 9780807579084

Papa wins a Thanksgiving turkey at work. The only problem is… it's a live turkey. Papa takes the turkey home with him on the subway. Mama's reaction: "A turkey doesn't belong in a fourth-floor walk-up!" The humorous tale is based on a true story.

Older Readers

***The Ship to Nowhere: On Board the Exodus* by Rona Arato.**
Second Story Press
ISBN: 9781772600186

In this work of historical fiction set in 1947 and based on actual events, eleven-year-old Rachel, her sister, and their mother are Jewish refugees aboard the Exodus taking them to Palestine. In view of land, the ship is detained by British warships and prevented from docking. The refugees' plight gained international attention and aid from caring individuals.

Irena's Children: Young Readers Edition: A True Story of Courage by Tilar J. Mazzeo.
Adapted by Mary Cronk Farrell.
Margaret K. McElderry Books, an imprint of Simon & Schuster
ISBN: 9781481449915

By the end of the Holocaust, Irena Sendler had rescued approximately 2,500 children from certain death. For her acts of bravery and selflessness, Yad Vashem named her "Righteous among the Nations" in 1965. Through skillful sensory details, Mazzeo leads the young reader to imagine what life was like in occupied Warsaw during World War II.

The Bicycle Spy by **Yona Zeldis McDonough.**
Scholastic Books
ISBN: 9780545850957

In a Frenchvillage in 1942, twelve-year-old Marcel joins the Resistance and delivers messages via bicycle to help his Jewish friends evade capture.

Skating with the Statue of Liberty by **Susan Lynn Meyer.**
Delacorte Press, an imprint of Random House
ISBN: 9780385741552

This sequel to *Black Radishes* (a 2011 Honor Award Winner) finds Gustave's family in New York, having escaped Occupied France. Gustav's friendship with September Rose, a young African American girl, helps him adjust to his family's new life as American immigrants.

Teen Readers

No Notable Books recognized.

2016 Awards

Younger Readers

Ketzel the Cat who Composed **by Lesléa Newman.**
Illustrations by Amy June Bates.
Candlewick Press
ISBN: 9780763665555

Inspired by a true story, this picture book tells the story of Moshe, a young composer who takes in a stray cat. Together, the two manage to create music in the most interesting way.

Older Readers

Adam and Thomas **by Aharon Appelfeld. Translated by Jeffrey M. Green.**
Illustrations by Phillipe Dumas.
Seven Stories Press
ISBN: 9781609806347

Adam and Thomas are two nine-year-old boys who must fend for themselves in the forest during World War II. With only minimal help, the boys live under harsh conditions, fighting for survival and experience small miracles.

Teen Readers

The Hired Girl **by Laura Amy Schlitz.**
Candlewick Press
ISBN: 9780763678180

After running away from her father who forbids education and burns her beloved books, fourteen-year-old Joan heads to Baltimore where she is hired as a maid for a Jewish family. Set in the early 1900s and told first person via diary entries, Joan dreams of love, learning and the future.

Honor Books

Younger Readers

Shanghai Sukkah **by Heidi Smith Hyde.**
Illustrations by Jing Jing Tsong.
Kar-Ben Publishing
ISBN: 9781467734745
To escape the war, Marcus and his family move from Berlin to China. With his new friend Liang, Marcus learns to celebrate Sukkot while embracing his new surroundings and Chinese customs.

Everybody Says Shalom **by Leslie Kimmelman.**
Illustrations by Talitha Shipman.
Random House
ISBN: 9780385383363

With colorful pictures and a helpful historical guide in the back, this rhyming picture book is a child-friendly tour guide of Israel.

Older Readers

Hereville: How Mirka Caught a Fish **by Barry Deutsch.**
Amulet Books, an imprint of Abrams Books
ISBN: 9781419708008

Yes, Mirka, the feisty eleven-year-old Orthodox girl is back with another adventure as scary as her first two: babysitting her step-sister Layele. This rather complicated yarn involves a magic troll (see *Hereville*, Book 1), who gives them a magic hairband that enables time travel; a witch (again, see *Hereville*, Book 1), who had interactions with Fruma, their mother in the past; a wishing fish and a seashell water charm.

Teen Readers

Stones on a Grave **by Kathy Kacer.**
Orca Book Publishers
ISBN: 9781459806597

It's 1964 and eighteen-year-old Sara, an orphan from Ontario, treks to Germany to unravel the truth about her Jewish parentage. This book is part of the Secrets series.

Serendipity's Footsteps by Suzanne Nelson.
Alfred A. Knopf, an imprint of Random House
ISBN: 9780385392129

Linked by a pair of shoes, this book chronicles the lives of three different girls throughout time and distance.

Notable Books
Younger Readers

Hanukkah Cookies with Sprinkles by David A. Adler.
Illustrations by Jeffrey Ebbeler.
Apple & Honey Press, an imprint of Behrman House & Gefen Publishing House
ISBN: 9781681155005

As Hanukkah approaches, Sarah learns the importance of *tzedakah,* helping those in need, friendship and kindness and Jewish tradition.

Sadie and Ori and the Blue Blanket by Jamie Korngold.
Illustrations by Julie Fortenberry.
Kar-Ben Publishing
ISBN: 9781467711920

Through the connection of a hand-knit blanket, this is a sweet story depicting the relationship between a grandmother and her two grandchildren throughout time.

The Parakeet Named Dreidel by Isaac Bashevis Singer.
Illustrations by Suzanne Raphael Berkson.
Farrar, Straus and Giroux
ISBN: 9780374300944

Unable to find its owners, David and his family are delighted to take in a Yiddish speaking parakeet they name Dreidel. Many years later, David connects to Dreidel's past in the most unexpected way.

Older Readers

The Safest Lie by Angela Cerrito.
Holiday House
ISBN: 9780823433100

Nine-year-old Anna struggles to conceal and relinquish her Jewish heritage when she must pose as a Catholic girl in order to escape the Warsaw Ghetto.

Mr. Doctor: Janusz Korczak and the Orphans of the Warsaw Ghetto by Irene Cohen-Janka.
Illustrations by Maurizio A. C. Quarello
ISBN: 9781554517152

Based on a true story, this illustrated book is about Janusz Korczak, a Polish doctor who cared for and housed and ultimately refused to abandon a group of Jewish children in the Warsaw Ghetto.

Watch Out for Flying Kids: How Two Circuses, Two Countries, and Nine Kids Confront Conflict and Build Community by Cynthia Levinson.
Peachtree Publishers
ISBN: 9781561458219

This non-fiction book takes readers behind the scenes of two traveling kid circuses. Unique social aspects are highlighted as the circuses include kids from a variety of different cultures, religions and races.

The Wren and the Sparrow by J. Lewis.
Illustrations by Yevgenia Nayberg.
Kar-Ben Publishing
ISBN: 9781467719513

Forced to surrender their musical instruments to the Nazis, this lyrical story is based on true events. It focuses on the story of a musician, his clever student and the miraculous preservation of a beloved hurdy-gurdy that withstands the war and sees through generations.

The Girl in the Torch by Robert Sharenow.
Balzer + Bray, an imprint of Harper Collins Publishers
ISBN: 9780062227959

After being denied entry at Ellis Island, twelve-year-old Sarah makes the brave decision to jump ship and make a home for herself inside the Statue of Liberty.

Teen Readers

Last Night at the Circle Cinema **by Emily Franklin.**
Carolrhoda Lab
ISBN: 9781467774895

On the eve of high school graduation, three best friends decide to spend the night in the Circle Cinema, an abandoned movie theater where they unravel secrets, cope with past struggles and triumphs and ultimately face the their futures.

Courage and Defiance: Stories of Spies, Saboteurs, and Survivors in World War II Denmark **by Deborah Hopkinson.**
Scholastic
ISBN: 9780545592208

This book chronicles the true stories of the brave people behind the Nazi resistance efforts and the countless lives they saved during the Holocaust.

Imagining Katherine **by Carol Solomon.**
Tova Press
ISBN: 9780692486481

Through high-schooler Katherine's eyes, the novel tackles topics such as racism, segregation, the civil rights movement and Jewish identity in the cultural climate of 1960s Baltimore.

Deep Sea **by Annika Thor.**
Translated by Linda Schenck.
Delacorte Press, an imprint of Penguin Random House
ISBN: 9780385743853

Three years earlier, Jewish sisters Stephie and Nellie were sent to live with foster families on a Swedish island. Now sixteen-years-old, Stephie deals with "typical" teen issues such as school and friends while grappling with the fact that her parents remain in an Austrian concentration camp. This is the third book about the Steiner Sisters.

2015 Awards

Younger Readers

My Grandfather's Coat by Jim Aylesworth.
Illustrations by Barbara McClintock.
Scholastic
ISBN: 9780439925457.

A delightful retelling of the Yiddish folksong "I Had a Little Overcoat," in which, the main character is a Jewish immigrant to the United States who works as a tailor. The descriptive illustrations expand on the narrative and weave their own tale of the man's life cycle events.

Older Readers

Hidden: A Child's Story of the Holocaust by Loïc Dauvillier.
Illustrations by Marc Lizano. Color by Greg Salsedo.
Translated by Alexis Siege.
First Second
ISBN: 9781596438736.

In graphic novel format, a grandmother recounts to her granddaughter her experiences as a hidden Jewish child in Nazi-occupied France during the Holocaust. The grey and brown-tinted illustrations portray a dark and scary time. However, the text and images provide a gentle introduction to the Holocaust for elementary grade and middle grade readers.

Teen Readers

Storm by Donna Jo Napoli.
Simon & Schuster Books for Young Readers
ISBN: 9781481403023.

A novel based on the Bible Story Noah's Ark told through the viewpoint of Sebah, a sixteen-year-old woman, who is a stowaway on the Ark. Sebah describes the severe conditions of the flood which took the lives of her family. Also, she shares her observations of the turmoil on the Ark between Noah and his family members as well as amongst the animals.

Honor Books

Younger Readers

Goldie Takes a Stand by Barbara Krasner.
Illustrations by Kelsey Garrity-Rile.
Kar-Ben Publishing
ISBN: 9781467712019
A young Golda Meir is the president of the American Young Sisters Society where she uses her leadership skills to raise money to purchase books for immigrant students.

Never Say a Mean Word Again: A Tale from Medieval Spain by Jacqueline Jules.
Illustrations by Durga Yael Bernhard.
Wisdom Tales
ISBN: 978-1937786-20-5.
A universal story of friendship and cross-cultural understanding based on a Spanish legend. Samuel's father, a Jewish vizier, advises Samuel after offends his friend Hamza and Hamza (son of the tax collector) responds with anger. Samuel's father says, "make sure Hamza never says a mean word to you again." As a result, Samuel and Hamsa begin to enjoy activities together, and their friendship grows in spite of their challenging beginnings.

Older Readers

Death by Toilet Paper by Donna Gephart.
Delacorte Press, an imprint of Penguin Random House
ISBN: 9780385743990.

Benjamin Epstein faces many challenges since his father's death most significantly, being evicted from his home. Benjamin does his best to help out his mom, by entering contests, including one for a toilet paper company slogan. When his aging grandfather moves in trouble escalates for Ben. Realistic, deeply touching, with just the right balance of kid friendly humor.

Whispering Town by Jennifer Elvgren.
Illustrations by Fabio Santomauro.
Kar-Ben Publishing
ISBN: 9781467711944.

A picture book for older readers set in 1943 Nazi-occupied Denmark. In a small fishing village Anette and her parents hide a Jewish mother and son in their cellar until they can travel safely to Sweden. Evocative illustrations add depth to the story.

Teen Readers

Isabel's War by Lila Perl.
Lizzie Skurnick Books, an imprint of IG Publishing
ISBN: 9781939601278

Isabel is a self- centered American girl who is not happy about having to spend her summer vacation in a resort with her parents. She is even more unhappy when she finds out she will have to share her room with Helga, a beautiful German girl. Gradually, Isabel learns what is happening to the Jews in Europe, that Helga was saved by the *Kindertransport*, and tries to learn the terrible secret Helga is keeping. The story integrates factual material about World War, the status of refugees, attitudes of Americans towards the German refugees and some the experiences of the Kindertransport children.

Like No Other by Una LaMarche.
Razor Bill, an imprint of Penguin Group
ISBN: 9781595146748

The story of a Hasidic girl, Devorah, who has a chance meeting in a hospital elevator, during a power out, with a young black teen named Jaxon. Contrary to Devorah's stereotype of black boys, Jaxon is respectful and tries to help them escape from the dark elevator. An unlikely friendship develops. Although they would both like their friendship to develop into something more, Devorah realizes that she does not want to give up her relationship with her family and her community, and they each must go on with their individual lives.

Notable Books

Younger Readers

Anna & Solomon by Elaine Snyder.
Illustrations by Harry Bliss.
Margaret Ferguson, an imprint of Farrar Strauss and Giroux
ISBN: 978-0374-303624.

Anna and Solomon were Russian Jews in the 1890's. They had only enough money for one ticket to America. Solomon sailed alone. He worked hard to save money for Anna to join him. As each of 3 ships dock in New York, various members of Anna's family disembark without Anna. Finally, Anna made the journey. The story is based on the author's grandparent's immigration experience.

Here is the World by Lesléa Newman.
Illustrations by Susan Gal.
Abrams Books for Young Readers
ISBN: 9781419711855

Here is a book of simple rhymes for each Jewish holiday (and a baby naming). Here is a custom to make the holiday come alive. Here are recipes or crafts to enrich the celebrations Here is a description of each holiday. Here is the repetition of the rhyme that will keep young children reading along with the text.

The Mitten String by Jennifer Rosner.
Illustrations by Kristina Swarner.
Random House Books for Young Readers
ISBN: 9780385371186

This is an original folktale about a girl who knits, a deaf woman, and a piece of blue yarn. Ruthie's family raise sheep and young Ruthie loves to knit mittens from the wool. Her family invites a deaf woman and her baby to spend the night. Ruthie wonders how the mother will hear the child during the night. Her discovery leads to an invention for not losing mittens.

Rabbi Benjamin's Buttons by Alice B. McGinty.
Illustrations by Jennifer Black Reinhardt.
Charlesbridge Publishing
ISBN: 9781580894326
Rabbi's Benjamin's Congregation give him a beautiful vest to wear on Jewish holidays. As he eats and eats the special foods (recipes included), the four silver buttons pop off . Over the summer, he loses the extra weight by helping his friends with physically active holiday preparations. Charming and colorful illustrations.

Simon and the Bear by Eric Kimmel.
Illustrations by Matthew Trueman.
Disney Hyperion
ISBN: 9781423143550

A zany and fun Hanukkah tale of Simon, a Russian boy on his way to America. After a shipwreck he is stranded on an iceberg. Simon is saved by a polar bear that shares his latkes, enjoys his songs, goes fishing for him and keeps him warm at night. Simon experiences miracle after miracle during his journey.

The Story of Passover by David Adler.
Illustrations by Jill Weber.
Holiday House
ISBN: 9780823429028.

A beautifully illustrated and accurate retelling of the children of Israel's journey from slavery in Egypt to freedom. Many of the "gruesome" parts of the story are included, such as the death of the firstborn child and the Egyptians drowning in the Red Sea.

Older Readers

Fleabrain Loves Franny by Joanne Rocklin.
Amulet Books, an imprint of Abrams Books
ISBN: 9781419710681.

In 1952 Pittsburgh, a young Jewish girl convalescing from polio is befriended by an erudite flea with supernatural powers. The book is both an engaging work of historical fiction and a highly imaginative animal fantasy.

From Foe to Friend & Other Stories: A Graphic Novel by S.Y. Agnon.
Illustrations by Shay Charka.
English language edition adapted by Jeffrey Saks.
The Toby Press
ISBN: 9781592643950

Charka's witty, approachable panel-art illustrations capture the essence of three tales by Nobel Prize laureate Agnon, who died in 1970. Themes include kindness, persistence, creativity, and Jewish mysticism.

I *Lived on Butterfly Hill* by Margorie Agosín.
Illustrated by Lee White.
Translated by E. M. O'Connor.
Atheneum Books for Young Readers
ISBN: 9781416953449

Eleven-year-old Celeste idyllic life in Valparíso—where her abuela settled after fleeing the Nazis—is violently upended with Chile's bloody coup d'état (here fictionalized). Agosin's lyrical writing—her sensory descriptions of Chile and sensitive portrayal of one girl's coming-of-age—is pure poetry.

Schools of Hope: How Julius Rosenwald Helped Change African American Education by **Norman H. Finkelstein.**
Calkins Creek
ISBN: 9781590788417

Inspired by Booker T. Washington, the president of Sears, Roebuck and Company, Julius Rosenwald, helped build over 5300 schools for African Americans in the segregated South. A well-researched account of one man's act of *tzedakah*, on a grand scale.

Teen Readers

Freedom Summer: The 1964 Struggle for Civil Rights in Mississippi by **Susan Goldman Rubin.**
Holiday House
ISBN: 9780823429202

Rubin commemorates the fiftieth anniversary of "Freedom Summer" with an informative look at events, including the tragic murders of three young civil rights workers. Her firsthand interviews bring immediacy and intimacy to history.

Gottika by **Helaine Becker.**
Illustrations by Alexander Griggs-Burr.
Dancing Cat Books
ISBN: 9781770863910

In a futuristic society, "Stoons"—a learned and peaceful people—are persecuted by the Nazi-like Gottikan rulers. Dany's father conjures a "gol" to protect their people. Dramatic interspersed panel illustrations help set the pace for this gripping tale.

Playing for the Commandant by **Suzy Zail.**
Candlewick Press
ISBN: 9780763664039

In Auschwitz, young pianist Hanna must perform for the Nazis to keep her mother and sister alive. She falls in love with the commandant's son, Karl, whose kindness in the face of horror helps sustain her.

Prisoner of Night and Fog by **Anne Blankman.**
Balzer + Bray, an imprint of HarperCollins Publishers
ISBN: 9780062278814.

In 1923 Munich, seventeen-year-old Gretchen, a favorite of "Uncle Dolph," has her eyes opened to the coming atrocities by a courageous young Jewish reporter. Taut mystery, engaging historical fiction, and romantic love story.

Rachel's Hope by Shelly Sanders.
Second Story Press
ISBN: 9781927583425.

This conclusion to the Rachel Trilogy, based on true events, finds the protagonist settling in to life in early-1900s San Francisco. Alternating chapters describe Sergei's flight from Siberian exile. The book's ending is cathartic, if heartbreaking.

2014 Awards

Younger Readers

The Longest Night: A Passover Story by Laurel Snyder.
Illustrations by Catia Chien.
Schwartz & Wade Books, an imprint of Random House Books
ISBN: 9780375969423

Written in gentle verse, the tumultuous days leading up to the Jews' flight from Egypt are described from the perspective of an unnamed slave girl in this beautifully illustrated story.

Older Readers

The Blessing Cup by Patricia Polacco.
Simon & Schuster Books for Young Readers
ISBN: 9781442450479.

The miraculous journey from the shtetl to America of the remaining teacup from a china tea set, deliberately left behind when her Jewish ancestors were forced to leave Czarist Russia, will strike an emotional chord with readers.

Teen Readers

The Nazi Hunters : How a Team of Spies and Survivors Captured the World's Most Notorious Nazi by **Neal Bascomb.**
Arthur A. Levine Books, an imprint of Scholastic
ISBN: 9780545430999.

A stunning account of the mission to capture Adolf Eichmann by an elite team of Israeli spies is dramatically brought to life.

Honor Books

Younger Readers

Rifka Takes a Bow by **Betty Rosenberg Perloy.**
Illustrations by Cosei Kawa.
Kar-Ben Publishing
ISBN: 9780761381273

A young girl shares her experiences being the daughter of performers in the Yiddish theater during the 1920's in New York City.

Stones for Grandpa by **Renee Londner.**
Illustrations by Martha Avilés.
Kar-Ben Publishing
ISBN: 9780761374954

The Jewish custom of placing stones on a gravestone is gently explained to young children, through the eyes of a young boy as he remembers his grandfather.

Older Readers

The Boy on the Wooden Box: How the Impossible Became Possible...on Schindler's List by **Leon Leyson with Marilyn J. Harran and Elisabeth B. Leyson.**
Atheneum Books for Young Readers
ISBN: 9781442497818

The late Leon Leyson has created an inspiring memoir about his experiences during the Holocaust. He was one of the youngest children on Oskar Schindler's list.

Dear Canada: Pieces of the Past: The Holocaust Diary of Rose Rabinowitz, Winnipeg, Manitoba, 1948 **by Carol Matas.**
Scholastic Canada
ISBN: 9781443113076

Rose's fictional diary depicts her struggle to adjust to a new life as an orphan in Canada after WWII and shares her horrific experiences during the war.

Teen Readers

Dancing in the Dark **by Robyn Bavati.**
Flux
ISBN: 9780738734774.

Ditty Cohen, an orthodox teen, is forced to keep her passion and talent for ballet dancing hidden from her family. She studies ballet in secret, but ultimately must choose between a life on the stage as a dancer and her family.

The War Within These Walls **by Aline Sax.**
Illustrations by Caryl Strzelecki.
Translated by Laura Watkinson.
Eerdmans Books for Young Readers
ISBN: 9780802854285

The appalling conditions of the Warsaw Ghetto. are shown in this unforgettable illustrated novel. The narrator, a teenage Jewish boy's, story begins with the invasion of Poland and dramatically shows the role the he plays in the Warsaw Ghetto Uprising.

Notable Books

Younger Readers

Benny's Mitzvah Notes **by Marc Lumer.**
Hachai Publishing
ISBN: 9781929628698

Benny, a young Orthodox Jewish boy, loves the mitzvah notes his parents make for him. Benny grows up and writes a touching mitzvah note of his own.

Brave Girl: Clara and the Shirtwaist Makers' Strike of 1909 by **Michelle Markel.**
Illustrations by Melissa Sweet.
Balzer & Bray, an imprint of HarperCollins Publishers
ISBN: 9780061804427

In 1909, Clara Lemlich and her fellow garment workers band together to create better conditions. With resilience and courage, young Clara stands up for what she believes.

The Cats on Ben Yehuda Street by **Ann Redisch Stampler.**
Illustrations by Francesca Carabelli.
Kar-Ben Publishing
ISBN: 9780761381235

Cranky fish shop owner Mr. Modiano and his neighbor Mrs. Spiegel are brought together in the most unlikely of ways with the help of two mischievous cats.

Hanukkah in Alaska by **Barbara Brown.**
Illustrations by Stacey Schuett.
Henry Holt and Company
ISBN: 9780805097481

A girl living in Alaska is frustrated when a moose won't leave her backyard, threatening to chomp down the tree holding up her beloved swing. Even the celebration of Hanukkah doesn't distract her.

The Passover Lamb by **Linda Elovitz Marshall.**
Illustrations by Tatjana Mai-Wyss.
Random House Children's Books
ISBN: 9780307931771

On the morning of Passover, Miriam discovers one of the sheep on her family's farm has given birth to triplets! Miriam has a clever plan to attend the Seder and celebrate Passover with the help of a baby lamb.

Our Special New Baby by **Chava Cohen.**
Illustrations by Rivkie Braverman.
Feldheim
ISBN: 9781598269604

Racheli's father explains that her new baby brother is very special. He was born with Down syndrome. Racheli and her siblings learn about understanding, acceptance, and love.

Older Readers

The Barefoot Book of Jewish Tales **by Shoshana Gelfand Boyd.**
Illustrations by Amanda Hall.
Story CD narrated by Debra Messing.
Barefoot Books
ISBN: 9781846868849

A charming collection of eight different stories, each tale highlights a Jewish value depicted in a child-friendly manner.

B.U.G. (Big Ugly Guy) **by Jane Yolen and Adam Stemple.**
Dutton's Children Books, an imprint of Penguin
ISBN: 9780525422389

Tired of being bullied, Sammy decides to build a golem out of clay for protection. The golem even becomes drummer in his band. But when the golem takes on a life of its own, Sammy must rethink his plan.

Odette's Secrets **by Maryann Macdonald.**
Bloomsbury Children's Books
ISBN: 9781599907505

After the Nazis invade Paris, Odette is sent to live with a Catholic family in the countryside. In order to stay safe, she must shed her Jewish identity. Based on a true story and told in free verse poetry, Macdonald tells the story of a young girl burdened by loss and secrets.

Touched by Fire **by Irene N. Watts.**
Tundra Books
ISBN: 9781770495241

An enthralling story of perseverance and strength, Watts depicts the chronology of Miriam and her family from 1905 when they flee the pogroms of Russia to their journey to reach Ellis Island and the tragedy of the Triangle Shirt Waist Fire.

When Hurricane Katrina Hit Home **by Gail Langer Karwoski.**
Illustrations by Julia Marshall.
The History Press
ISBN: 9781626190832

Although they come from two very different backgrounds, Chazz and Lyric are both affected when Hurricane Katrina roars through New Orleans. Told in alternating points of view, the children realize what is important in the aftermath of a storm that has changed their lives.

Teen Readers

Helga's Diary: A Young Girl's Account of Life in a Concentration Camp by **Helga Weiss.**
Translated by Neil Bermel.
W.W. Norton & Company
ISBN: 9780393077971

Cemented in a brick wall and miraculously retrieved after the war, Helga's real-life diary depicts her experiences in Terezin. With updated with family photos, footnotes, recollections, Helga's childhood drawings, journal entries, and diagrams, the bravery of a young girl during such a perilous time is illuminated.

Lauren Yanofsky Hates the Holocaust by **Leanne Lieberman.**
Orca Book Publishers
ISBN: 9781459801097
Seventeen-year-old Lauren doesn't want to be Jewish anymore. She is tired of Holocaust memoirs and Jewish summer camps. She believes Judaism is all about sadness, persecution, and loss. But when her friends start playing Nazi War games, Lauren realizes that her heritage is more important than she realized.

2013 Awards

Younger Readers

Hannah's Way by **Linda Glaser.**
Illustrations by Adam Gustavson.
Kar-Ben Publishing
ISBN: 9780761351382

When Hannah's teacher tries to arrange carpools for a Saturday class picnic, she is in a quandary. She cannot ride on the Sabbath, but she neither wants to miss the picnic nor draw attention to her Jewish heritage. Well researched illustrations with details of rural northern Minnesota during the Depression Era complement the story of how a child does not have to give up his or her heritage in order to fit in, a message that serves contemporary populations as well.

Older Readers

His Name Was Raoul Wallenberg by Louise Borden.
Houghton Mifflin Books for Children
ISBN: 978-0618507559

Borden's biography of the Swedish hero of Hungarian Jewry during World War II has all the hallmarks of excellent non-fiction: extensive research, lists of sources, and prose and visual materials that make a complicated chapter of history easily accessible.

Teen Readers

Intentions by Deborah Heiligman.
Knopf Books for Young Readers, a division of Random House
ISBN: 9780375868610

When Rachel overhears an encounter between her rabbi and a female congregant in the synagogue sanctuary, her world starts unraveling as she questions whom she can trust. She evaluates her relationships with parents, friends, and the rabbi, and learns about her own motivations in the process. Well-developed characters and authentic voice emphasize the many nuances of the title.

Honor Books
Younger Readers

Zayde Comes to Live by Sheri Sinykin.
Illustrations by Kristina Swarner.
Peachtree Publishers
ISBN: 978-1561456314

A "poignant, powerful, sweet" story of a girl and her grandfather that deals with death and the afterlife from a Jewish perspective.

The Elijah Door: A Passover. Tale by Linda Leopold Strauss.
Illustrations by Alexi Natchev.
Holiday House
ISBN: 978-0823419111

Next door neighbors Rachel Galinsky and David Lippa are in love, but their families are feuding. With spring in the air, Passover preparations and some help from the rabbi, "it takes a village" to bring the couple together. The *shtetl* is brought to life with vibrant woodcuts and a definite Yiddish cadence to the text.

Older Readers

***The Wooden Sword: A Jewish Folktale from Afghanistan* by Ann Redisch Stampler.**
Illustrations by Carol Liddiment.
Albert Whitman & Company
ISBN: 978-0807592014

A shoemaker's faith that everything will turn out as it should is tested by the Afghan shah, who forces him to work as a water carrier, woodcutter and soldier. But when the shoemaker is asked to do a beheading, his own cleverness saves the day. Colorful, detailed illustrations lend a strong sense of place.

Teen Readers

***Beyond Courage: The Untold Story of Jewish Resistance during the Holocaust* by Doreen Rappaport**
Candlewick Press
ISBN: 978-0763629762

The authors presents "a sampling of actions, efforts, and heroism with the hope that [she] can play a role in helping to correct the damaging and persistent belief that Jews 'went like sheep to the slaughter.'" Five years of research results in an important informational book, with back matter that includes a pronunciation guide, chronology, source notes, detailed bibliography, and an index.

Notable Books
Younger Readers

***Speak Up, Tommy!* by Jacqueline Dembar Greene.**
Illustrations by Deborah Melmon.
Kar-Ben Publishing
ISBN: 9780761374978

Inspired by real events, Tommy's classmates stop teasing him about his Israeli accent when he helps the policeman manage his Israeli-trained dog.

***Sadie and the Big Mountain* by Jamie Korngold.**
Illustrations by Julie Fortenberry.
Kar-Ben Publishing
ISBN: 9780761364948

Sadie's synagogue preschool is spending the week preparing for Shavuot, the culmination of which will be a mountain hike similar to Moshe ascending Mount Sinai. Sadie does not like hiking, and she imagines getting sick with different ailments so she won't have to go.

***A Sweet Passover* by Lesléa Newman.**
Illustrations by David Slonim.
Abrams Books for Young Readers
ISBN: 9780810997370

By the last day of Passover, Miriam has had her fill of *matzah*. But as the family recounts why Jews eat *matzah* on Passover, she is convinced and tries her grandfather's *matzah brei*. Recipe included.

***The Schmutzy Family* by Madelyn Rosenberg.**
Illustrations by Paul Meisel.
Holiday House
ISBN: 9780823423712

All week the family discovers new ways to get dirty and the mother is never flustered. But when Shabbat comes, it's time to clean up.

***A Song for My Sister* by Lesley Simpson.**
Illustrations by Tatjana Mai-Wyss.
Random House Books for Young Readers
ISBN: 9781582464275

Mira longed for a little sister, but she didn't realize how much noise a baby could make, or the big changes to family life. When the baby cries the day of her *simchat bat* (baby naming), Mira calms her with a song.

Older Readers

***Hereville: How Mirka Met a Meteorite* by Barry Deutsch.**
Amulet Books, an imprint of Abrams
ISBN: 9781419703980

That plucky, knitting, Sabbath-observing heroine is back with another adventure that involves a meteorite, an evil twin, and a witch.

Small Medium at Large by **Joanne Levy.**
Bloomsbury USA Children
ISBN: 9781599908366

At her mother's wedding reception, Lilah is struck by lightning, which enables her to communicate with the dead. With the help of her grandmother and various other spirits, Lilah is able to overcome her shyness and help others.

Looking for Me by **Betsy R. Rosenthal.**
Houghton Mifflin Books for Children.
ISBN: 9780547610849

Written in free verse about the author's mother, who grew up as the fourth child of twelve in Baltimore during the 1930's, this book explores her challenges of being her own person while getting along with her siblings.

Teen Readers

Now by **Morris Gleitzman.**
Henry Holt and Company
ISBN: 9780805093780.

Felix is now a retired doctor and grandfather in the final book of this award-winning trilogy (*Once* and *Then*, Honor Books in 2011 and 2012, respectively). It is narrated by his granddaughter, Zelda, who deals with the absence of working parents, bullying, and raging fires in Australia.

Rachel's Secret by **Shelly Sanders.**
Second Story Press
ISBN: 9780926920375

The Kishiniev riots of 1903 are the basis for a story of love and friendship as Rachel and Sergei grow closer amid the tension and anti-Semitism of pre-Revolutionary Russia.

The Last Song by **Eva Wiseman.**
Tundra Books
ISBN: 9780887769795
Isabel dislikes her intended husband, but her parents hope to protect her from the dangers of the Inquisition by marrying her off to the scion of an important

Catholic family. As Isabel discovers her Jewish roots, she rights to save her family in this historical fiction.

2012 Awards

Younger Readers

Chanukah Lights by Michael J. Rosen.
Artwork by Robert Sabuda.
Candlewick Press
ISBN: 9780763655334

Simple text combines with amazing pop-ups to tell the story of Chanukah from its origins in the Temple throughout history and the world. A page for each night, including depictions of a ship and a skyscraper, will delight readers of all ages.

Older Readers

Music Was It: Young Leonard Bernstein by Susan Goldman Rubin.
Charlesbridge Publishing
ISBN: 9781580893442

A chronicle of the pianist/composer/conductor's early life – from his childhood in Boston to his conducting debut at Carnegie Hall, is full of photographs, direct quotes, and interesting anecdotes. The excellent back matter includes biographies of famous associates, a discography, bibliography, and an index.

Teen Readers

The Berlin. Boxing Club by Robert Sharenow.
Harper Teen, an imprint of HarperCollins
ISBN: 9780061579684

Karl Stern, an assimilated fourteen-year-old Jew living in 1930s Berlin, becomes the unlikely student of boxing champion and source of German pride, Max Schmeling. A coming of age novel that entwines Karl's personal struggles with the historical ones of the period including "degenerate" art and the Nazi menace, well-developed characters and a tense plot propel this page turner.

Honor Books

Younger Readers

Naamah and the Ark at Night by **Susan Campbell Bartoletti.**
Illustrations by Holly Meade.
Candlewick Press
ISBN: 9780763642426

Using an extremely disciplined poetry form, Bartoletti crafts a lullaby about Naamah, Noah's wife, calming the animals at night with her singing. Meade's lush, dramatic artwork brings the inhabitants of the ark to life.

Around the World in One Shabbat by **Durga Yael Bernhard.**
Jewish Lights Publishing
ISBN: 9781580234337

Starting Friday afternoon in the Jerusalemmarketplace, author/illustrator Bernhard circles the globe through Argentina, Australia, Turkey, Russia, France, America, Ethiopia, Germany, Canada, Morocco, Thailand, and India to explore the different customs and rituals of the Sabbath. Havdalah is recited in a home near the *Kotel*, as the trip around the world is complete. Colorful ovals of activity accompany the descriptive narrative.

Older Readers

Lily Renee, Escape Artist: from Holocaust Survivor to Comic Book Pioneer **by Trina Robbins.**
Illustrations by Anne Timmons and Mo Oh.
Graphic Universe, an imprint of Lerner Publishing
ISBN: 9780761381143

Not only did Lily Wilheim survive, she triumphed over circumstances that forced her from a loving home in pre-war Vienna, on a *Kindertransport* to England, to the United States and through a variety of jobs and situations to become a comic book illustrator. Timmons and Oh's vibrant graphic format, and the back matter with photographs, a glossary and historical descriptions, make for an exciting and educational biography.

Hammerin' Hank Greenberg: Baseball Pioneer by **Shelley Sommer.**
Calkins Creek, an imprint of Boyds Mills Press
ISBN: 9781590784525

Sommer's biography follows Greenberg's achievements on and off the baseball field, including the challenges of anti-Semitism and parental disapproval of professional sports.

***Irena's Jars of Secrets* by Marcia Vaughan.**
Illustrations by Ron Mazellan.
Lee & Low Books
ISBN: 9781600604393

Polish social worker (and Righteous Gentile) Irena Sendler rescued over 2,500 children from the Warsaw Ghetto. The story of her bravery and quiet heroism is complemented by Mazellan's somber-toned, expressive illustrations.

Teen Readers

***Then* by Morris Gleitzman.**
Henry Holt and Company
ISBN: 9780805090277

Continuing where 2011 Honor Book *Once* left off, Felix tells how he and Zelda find refuge in a Polish farm village, but must still use quick thinking and imagination to survive the degradations of the Holocaust.

***The Blood Lie* by Shirley Reva Vernick.**
Cinco Puntos Press
ISBN: 9781933693842

Inspired by a real blood libel that took place in upstate New York in 1928, Jack Pool's promising career as a cellist is jeopardized when a young girl disappears in the woods and he is accused of murdering her for a Jewish blood ritual.

Notable Books

Younger Readers

***Picnic at Camp Shalom* by Jacqueline Jules.**
Illustrations by Deborah Melmon.
Kar-Ben Publishing
ISBN: 9780761366614

Carly and Sara become fast friends during activity-filled days of camp, but there is also a lesson to be learned about dealing with friends and trying to make things right after a misunderstanding.

The Golem's Latkes by Eric A. Kimmel.
Illustrations by Aaron Jansinski.
Marshall Cavendish Children's Books
ISBN: 9780761459040

Hanukkah is a busy time for Rabbi Judah Loew and his household. The housemaid tasks the Maharal's Golem to keep making potato pancakes until she returns. When she loses track of time and the streets start to overflow, it turns into a latke party for the whole city. Acrylic on wood illustrations gives dimension to the man of clay and Prague.

Joseph and the Sabbath Fish by Eric A. Kimmel.
Illustrations by Martina Peluso.
Kar-Ben Publishing
ISBN: 9780761359081

Joseph is a poor man who spends his meager budget to honor the Sabbath by welcoming guests and serving delicacies. His neighbor, a wealthy merchant, is worried that Joseph will gain his riches. The merchant converts his holdings into one large gem, which ends up in the water. When local fishermen net a large beautiful fish, they know Joseph will buy it. When Joseph cuts it open, he finds the neighbor's jewel, and both learn the lesson from the Talmud (Shabbat 119a): if someone provides money for the benefit of the Sabbath, the Sabbath will more than repay him.

Sadie's Sukkah Breakfast by Jamie Korngold.
Illustrations by Julie Fortenberry.
Kar-Ben Publishing
ISBN: 9780761356479

Sadie and Ori wake up early and decide to eat in the sukkah. After schlepping all the food and utensils outside, they decide breakfast would be nicer with guests, so they bring out their stuffed animals.

The Shabbat Princess by Amy Meltzer.
Illustrations by Martha Avilés.
Kar-Ben Publishing
ISBN: 9780761351429

While Sabbath is often referred to as a "queen," Rosie channels her obsession with princesses to make sure her family's Shabbat is worthy of royalty.

Lipman Pike: America's First Home Run King by Richard Michelson. Illustrations by Zachary Pullen.
Sleeping Bear Press
ISBN: 9781585364657

What's a nice Jewish boy doing playing baseball? This picture-book biography follows Pike from his father's store in Brooklyn through his rise to fame as the first paid baseball player in America.

The Littlest Mountain by Barb Rosenstock. Illustrations by Melanie Hall.
Kar-Ben Publishing
ISBN: 9780761344957

God determines that the world needs rules, and He decides to "speak" from a mountain. But which mountain should it be? Mount Carmel is beautiful, Mount Hermon has three peaks, Mount Tabor is majestic, and Mount Gilboa has flower-filled meadows. According to the *Midrash Rabbah* (*Bereshit* 99:1), God chooses little" Mount Sinai because its unassuming and humble bearing is deemed the perfect spot. Hall's vibrant color illustrations give each mountain a distinct "personality."

I Will Come Back to You: A Family in Hiding during World War II by Marisabina Russo.
Schwartz & Wade Books, an imprint of Random House
ISBN: 9780375966958

A grandmother's (Nonna) charm bracelet tells the story of life in Italy before World War II and subsequent events that led to Nonna's immigration to America. A donkey, a piano, a bicycle, and piglets all play a part. Gouache-painted illustrations and vintage photographs on the endpapers add visual context.

Marcel Marceau: Master of Mime by Gloria Spielman. Illustrations by Manon Gauthier.
Kar-Ben Publishing
ISBN: 9780761339618

This beautiful picture book details the famous mime's lifelong love of performing, as well as his Jewish heritage and role in the French resistance during World War II.

One Little Chicken by Elka Weber.
Illustrations by Elisa Kleven.
Tricycle Press
ISBN: 9781582463742

Leora is thrilled to find a chicken in her yard. Her mother reminds her that "finders aren't keepers," even if the result is caring for a yard full of livestock until the owner can be found. Vibrant colors and varied page layouts illustrate the story based on Talmudic discussions of returning lost items.

Older Readers

The Mishkan: Its Structure and Its Sacred Vessels **by Rabbi Avrohom Biderman.**
Artscroll/Mesorah Publications
ISBN: 9781422610749

The intricacies and significance of the Tabernacle are "now vividly brought to life in a masterpiece of imagery, insight, and detail."

Flesh & Blood So Cheap: The Triangle Fire and Its Legacy **by Albert Marrin.**
Alfred A. Knopf, an imprint of Random House
ISBN: 9780375868894

One hundred years after the tragedy, Marrin uses the event as a focal point to discuss immigration, unions, and life in early 20th century New York City.

The Cats in the Doll Shop **by Yona Zeldis McDonough.**
Illustrations by Heather Maione.
Viking, an imprint of Penguin
ISBN: 9780670012794

The Breittlemann sisters, who were introduced in *The Doll Shop Downstairs* (Viking, 2009), have new adventures when their cousin Tania emigrates from Russia and they help some stray cats that are being mistreated.

When Life Gives You O.J. **by Erica S. Perl.**
Knopf Books for Young Readers, an imprint of Random House
ISBN: 978037585923

Zelly Fried desperately wants a dog. Her grandfather, Ace, suggests that Zelly shows how responsible she can be by taking care of a practice dog -- an empty orange juice container. In the process, Zelly learns a lot about loyalty, friendship, and being true to herself.

Irena Sendler and the Children of the Warsaw Ghetto by Susan Goldman Rubin.
Illustrations by Bill Farnsworth.
Holiday House
ISBN: 9780823422517

The story of the Polish woman who defied the Nazis and risked her life to save Jewish children is brought to life with detailed narrative and expressive, colorful paintings.

Terezin: Voices from the Holocaust by Ruth Thomson.
Candlewick Press
ISBN: 9780763649630

Using present-day and archival photographs, pictures of daily life created by internees, and artifacts, a chronological history of the infamous concentration camp captures both the eye and the reader's interest.

Teen Readers

Requiem: Poems of the Terezin Ghetto by Paul B. Janeczko.
Candlewick Press
ISBN: 9780763647378

"Solemn songs to the memory of the people who died within the walls of Theresienstadt" is how the author describes his works of sparse, yet powerful poetry. The book includes art created in the concentration camp, as well as historical notes and related resources.

OyMG by Amy Fellner Dominy.
Walker & Company, an imprint of Bloomsbury
ISBN: 9780802721778

Ellie Taylor hopes her debating skills will get her a scholarship to a prestigious Christian-affiliated private school. She attends summer speech camp and falls for Devon, a cute *shaygetz* whose grandmother happens to be the anti-Semitic sponsor of the scholarship. With some nudging from her *zaydeh* Ellie faces her toughest argument as she must decide between the scholarship and her Jewish identity.

2011 Awards

Younger Readers

Gathering Sparks by Howard Schwartz.
Illustrations by Kristina Swarner.
Roaring Brook Press, an imprint of Macmillan Children's Publishing Group
ISBN: 9781596432802

Dreamy, nature-filled watercolor, gouache, and pastel paintings beautifully illustrate the Jewish concept of *tikkun olam*, or repairing the world, through an intimate dialogue between a grandchild and grandfather. While based on the ancient mystical teaching of the famous sixteenth century Rabbi Isaac Luria, the gentle, inspiring text and soothing illustrations are accessible to readers of all faiths.

Older Readers

Hereville: How Mirka Got Her Sword by Barry Deutsch.
Amulet Books, an imprint of Abrams
ISBN: 9780810984226

Eleven year-old Mirka, living in a contemporary Orthodox community, has more on her mind than learning the "womanly arts" her stepmother insists she acquire. She is on a quest to find a sword and slay a dragon, when she encounters witches, trolls, a vicious pig, and a ghost along the way. Computer generated illustrations in a muted palette create an amusing and refreshing graphic novel adventure.

Teen Readers

The Things a Brother Knows by Dana Reinhardt.
Wendy Lamb Books, an imprint of Random House
ISBN: 9780375844553

When Levi's older brother Boaz makes an uncharacteristic decision to join the Marines, his Israeli-American family is shocked. He returns safely but hardly speaks to anyone and barely leaves his room. When Boaz claims he is going on a hiking trip, Levi follows him on a journey from Boston to Washington, DC on foot and comes to understand the depth of his brother's pain, and his love and loyalty for his family.

Honor Books

Younger Readers

Modeh Ani: A Good Morning Book by Sarah Gershman.
Illustrations by Kristina Swarner.
EKS Publishing
ISBN: 9780939144648

A lyrical interpretation of a selection of Morning Blessings taken from the *Birchot HaShachar* and written with a simplicity and elegance that can be understood by young listeners and readers. The illustrations are full of emotion, expressing the mystery of the dawn, the innocence of a child, the warmth of family, and the excitement and awe of facing each new day.

Emma's Poem: The Voice of the Statue of Liberty by Linda Glaser.
Illustrations by Claire. Nivola.
Houghton Mifflin Books for Children
ISBN: 9780547171845

This beautiful blending of words and pictures explores the life of Emma Lazarus and her work as a writer and humanitarian, focusing on her inspiring words of poetry in "The New Colossus" which would become the permanent inscription for the Statue of Liberty.

Cakes and Miracles: A Purim Tale by Barbara Diamond Goldin.
Illustrations by Jaime Zollars.
Marshall Cavendish Children
ISBN: 9780761457015

Young, blind Hershel wishes he could help his widowed mother more. When an angel appears in his dream, Hershel finds that he has special gifts he can use to help his mother bake for the Jewish holiday of Purim. Rich, full-spread illustrations in collage and acrylic paint warmly depict the Eastern European shtetl setting with expression and dimension in this update of the 1991 classic.

Older Readers

Resistance by Carla Jablonski.
Illustrations by Leland Purvis.
First Second, an imprint of Macmillan Children's Publishing Group
ISBN: 9781596432918

Paul must help his family run their hotel while his father is being held by the Nazi authorities. But when his best friend Henri, who is Jewish, escapes a roundup and is left behind, Paul and his sister decide to hide him and help him escape with the French Resistance. A graphic novel that provides a cinematic story of prejudice, fear, courage, and bold ingenuity.

One Is Not a Lonely Number by Evelyn Krieger.
YM Books
ISBN: 9780984162420

As an only child, Talia is an anomaly at her Jewish day school, where large families are the norm. When a young woman stays for an extended visit, Talia is forced to share her family and her home. Talia's journey toward understanding herself, her parents, and her friends is guided by her Jewish morals and values providing a positive and authentic portrayal of the contemporary Orthodox community for readers of all backgrounds.

Black Radishes by Susan Lynn Meyer.
Delacorte Press, an imprint of Random House Children's Books
ISBN: 9780385738811

Shortly before France is invaded, Gustave and his parents flee Paris for the countryside. Lonely for the friends he left behind, Gustave also faces anti-Semitism at school and an uncertain future while the family waits for visas to immigrate to America. Action, tension, and well developed characters coupled with compelling details and beautifully crafted prose create a detailed picture of life for Jewish families in France during World War II.

Teen Readers

Hush by Eishes Chayil.
Walker & Company, a division of Bloomsbury Publishing
ISBN: 9780802720887

Eight years after her best friend hangs herself, Gittel breaks her silence and risks her own reputation, and that of her family, to come forward to the police with the real reason that led to the suicide. Written anonymously by a former member of a Chassidic sect in Brooklyn, the story painfully and vividly reveals the ongoing effects of incest and molestation on the victim, as well as on friends, family, and the community.

Once by Morris Gleitzman.
Henry Holt and Company
ISBN: 9780805090260

The brutality and devastation of the Holocaust is shown through a Polish orphan named Felix and his experiences after he runs away from the orphanage where he lived for almost four years. Believing that his parents might still be alive, he tries to find them at their family-owned bookstore only to discover that his town no longer has any Jews still living in it and all the books in his family shop are gone.

Life, After by Sarah Darer Littman.
Scholastic
ISBN: 9780375844553

Daniella Bensimon's comfortable world in Buenos Ares, Argentina is slipping away after the country spirals into an economic meltdown. Faced with increasing economic distress and personal loss, the family makes the difficult decision to emigrate and struggles to adjust to their new life in New York.

Notable Books
Younger Readers

Engineer Ari and the Sukkah Express by Deborah Bodin Cohen.
Illustrations by Shahar Kober.
Kar-Ben Publishing
ISBN: 9780761351269

Engineer Ari, the first conductor of the new train from Jaffa to Jerusalem, builds a Sukkah using leftover wood and other materials gathered from friends along his route. When the Sukkah is complete, Ari and his friends figure out how to share it with everyone who contributed -- by turning one of the train cars into the Sukkah Express!

Feivel's Flying Horses by Heidi Smith Hyde.
Illustrations by Johanna van der Sterre.
Kar-Ben Publishing
ISBN: 9780761339571

A wood carver of synagogue arks and Torah scrolls uses his talents to create magnificent carousel horses on Coney Island. By the time the carousel is complete, he has earned enough money to bring his family to America.

Miriam in the Desert by Jacqueline Jules.
Illustrations by Natascia Ugliano.
Kar-Ben Publishing
ISBN: 9780761344940

Bezalel, the artist chosen by God to build the Holy Ark, is represented here as Miriam's grandson, who plays a crucial role in developing a new spiritual future for the Jews. Miriam offers encouragement and guidance to the weary Israelites as they continue their journey through the desert after they escape slavery in Egypt.

The Little Red Hen and the Passover Matzah by Leslie Kimmelman.
Illustrations by Paul Meisel.
Holiday House
ISBN: 9780823419524

The Little Red Hen wants to make *matzah* for Passover and hopes her friends will help. Just like in the familiar story, Sheep, Horse, and Dog flatly refuse. But, remembering the words from the Haggadah, "Let all who are hungry come and eat," Little Red Hen welcomes her friends to her Seder. And after the meal, guess who does the dishes?

Say Hello, Lily by Deborah Lakritz.
Illustrations by Martha Avilés.
Kar-Ben Publishing
ISBN: 9780761345114
Although shy at first, Lily becomes a regular volunteer at the Shalom House, a "place for older people to live if they need extra help," and performs a *mitzvah* when she chooses to celebrate her birthday with the residents.

Beautiful Yetta, the Yiddish Chicken by Daniel Pinkwater.
Illustrations by Jill Pinkwater.
Feiwel & Friends, an imprint of Macmillan
ISBN: 9780312558246

In a tri-lingual story, utilizing English, Yiddish, and Spanish, a brave and clever fowl is determined not to become Friday night's dinner. But poor, Yiddish speaking Yetta is homesick and lonely in Brooklyn, New York, until she gains new friends and a family among the Spanish speaking parrots on the telephone wires.

A Tale of Two Seders by Mindy Avra Portnoy.
Illustrations by Valeria Cis.
Kar-Ben Publishing
ISBN: 9780882599074

A young girl describes the six Passover meals that she has shared with her divorced parents over the last three years when the *charoset*, the traditional dish of apples, nuts, cinnamon, and wine, never tastes quite right. When her parents surprise her by joining together at the synagogue's community Seder, the girl realizes that her family is special in its own way.

Jackie's Gift by **Sharon Robinson.**
Illustrations by E. B. Lewis.
Viking, an imprint of Penguin
ISBN: 9780670011629

Steve Satlow is shocked when his favorite baseball hero, Jackie Robinson, moves onto his street. When Jackie discovers that Steve's family does not have a Christmas tree, he decides to surprise the family with one, not realizing they are Jewish. The author, Robinson's daughter, wrote the story in the hopes that it will "inspire families for generations to come to look beyond race and religion and into people's hearts."

Zishe the Strong Man by **Robert Rubenstein.**
Illustrations by Woody Miller.
Kar-Ben Publishing
ISBN: 9780761339588

A picture book biography that recounts the true-life story of Siegmund Breitbart, or Zishe, a young Polish Jew, who went from a tiny village to touring the world demonstrating great feats of physical strength including hauling a wagonload of ten men with his teeth for a half a mile down Fifth Avenue.

Sara Finds a Mitzva by **Rebeka Simhaee.**
Illustrations by Michael Weber.
Hachai   Publishing
ISBN: 9781929628469

When Sara finds a lost stuffed toy, her grandmother helps her perform the *mitzva* of returning lost articles. A series of clues, including a candy wrapper, a receipt, and a birthday hat, lead Sara to the toy's owner.

Baxter, the Pig Who Wanted to be Kosher by **Laurel Snyder.**
Illustrations by David Goldin.
Tricycle Press
ISBN: 9781582463155

Baxter desperately wants to experience Shabbat dinner, but is devastated when he learns that, according to Jewish law, pork is a forbidden food. He stuffs his face with kosher pickles and raisin challah, hoping to become kosher and even tries to become a cow. When a kind rabbi sets him straight, inviting him to spend Shabbat with her, Baxter realizes that it is much better to be a guest than an item on the menu.

The Rooster Prince of Breslov by Ann Redisch Stampler.
Illustrations by Eugene Yelchin.
Clarion Books, an imprint of Houghton Mifflin Harcourt
ISBN: 9780618989744

When the prince rips off his clothes and insists on crouching on the floor, crowing like a rooster, the kind and queen offer a bag of gold to anyone who can cure him. The doctor, the magicians, and the sorcerers all fail. Yet a frail old man with a very peculiar plan turns the rooster prince into a real mensch, full of compassion and ready to become a wise and benevolent king.

Dear Tree by Rivka Doba Weber.
Illustrations by Phyllis Saroff.
Hachai Publishing,
ISBN: 9781929628483

On Tu B'Shvat, the birthday of the tree, a young boy simply and sweetly states his wishes for the trees in the coming year including rain, blossoms, and fruit.

Older Readers

Is It Night or Day? by Fern Schumer Chapman.
Farrar Straus and Giroux, an imprint of Macmillan
ISBN: 9780374177447

Based on the author's mother's experiences, this is an honest and moving account of a twelve-year-old girl who leaves her parents behind to travel to American with the assistance of the One Thousand Children Project, a group whose goal was to rescue German children during the Holocaust.

Kings and Carpenters: One Hundred Bible Land Jobs You Might Have Praised or Panned by Laurie Coulter.
Illustrations by Mary Newbigging.
Annick Press
ISBN: 9781554512263

Offering a wealth of information about life in biblical times, this book focuses on jobs and the people who performed them in a fun and friendly format, peppered with illustrations and interesting graphics.

Hot Pursuit: Murder in Mississippi **by Stacia Deutsch and Rhody Cohon.**
Illustrations by Craig Orback.
Kar-Ben Publishing
ISBN: 9780761339557

The authors offer an age-appropriate account of Mikey Schwerner, Andrew Goodman, and James Chauncey, three young civil rights activists, who were murdered in Mississippi in the summer of 1964.

The Orphan Rescue **by Anne Dublin.**
Illustrations by Qin Leng.
Second Story Press
ISBN: 9781897187814

In 1937, after the death of their parents, Miriam and David live with their grandparents in Poland. Unable to care for them, David is brought to the Jewish Orphanage of Sosnoweic and Miriam is forced to quit school to help support the family. But when David is sold to a cruel man who puts him to work in a factory, it is up to Miriam to rescue him and reveal the truth about the orphanage director.

The Year of Goodbyes **by Debbie Levy.**
Hyperion Books/Disney
ISBN: 9781423129011

Jutta Salzberg is a typical German teen who shares her thoughts and feelings with her friends in their special albums, called *poesiealbums*. Through real entries, drawings and personal messages, coupled with emotive verse, readers see the events of Hitler's reign and the impact it had on families and communities.

Sharing Our Homeland: Palestinian and Jewish Children at Summer Peace Camp **by Trisha Marx.**
Photographs by Cindy Karp.
Lee & Low Books
ISBN: 9781584302605

This photographic essay presents the experiences of a group of Palestinian and Jewish children attending a summer peace camp together in Israel through the eyes of Alya, a Palestinian girl and Yuval, a Jewish boy.

Mitzvah the Mutt by Sylvia Rouss.
Illustrations by Martha Rast.
Yaldah Publishing
ISBN: 9781592871803

Mitzvah the Mutt narrates his experiences celebrating Shabbat, Hanukkah, and Passover with his adoptive Jewish family. He mistakes a *matzah* ball for a tennis ball, accidentally eats horseradish, and shakes water all over Bubbie to share his bath.

Teen Readers

An Unspeakable Crime: The Prosecution and Persecution of Leo Frank by **Elaine Marie Alphin.**
Carolrhoda Books, an imprint of Lerner
ISBN: 9780822589440

Utilizing primary sources such as newpaper articles, photographs and excerpts from letters, the author recounts the story of Leo Frank, who was unjustly accused and tried for the murder of thirteen-year-old Mary Phagan in 1913 Atlanta, and was ultimately lynched.

Annexed **by Sharon Dogar.**
Houghton Mifflin Books for Children
ISBN: 9780547501956

While Anne Frank's story is well known, what about Peter Van Pels, the teenage boy who hid with her? This fictionalized account begins in the Mauthausen concentration camp as Peter reflects back on his life in the Annex and his romantic relationship with the iconic diarist.

Inconvenient **by Margie Gelbwasser.**
Flux, an imprint of Llewellyn Worldwide
ISBN: 9780738721484

Russian-Jewish culture in America is the backdrop for an emotional story of how fifteen-year-old Alyssa copes with her mother's alcohol addiction while dealing with typical teenage issues such as friendship, underage drinking, and first love.

Anne Frank: The Anne Frank House Authorized Graphic Biography by **Sid Jacobson and Ernie Colón.**
Hill and Wang
ISBN: 9780809026852

This graphic novel offers a new perspective on Anne Frank's life and legacy beginning with her parents' childhoods and marriage and concluding with the publication of her diary and the effects it has had on the world.

Queen of Secrets by **Jenny Meyerhoff.**
Farrar Straus Giroux, an imprint of Macmillan
ISBN: 9780374326289

Loosely based on the story of Queen Esther, contemporary Essie is poised to have an amazing sophomore year when she makes the cheerleading squad and captures the attention of Austin, the captain of the football team. But things get complicated when her religious cousin Micah moves back to town and becomes a target of anti-Semitism, bullying and hazing by members of the football team.

Under a Red Sky: Memoir of a Childhood in Communist Romania by **Haya Leah Molnar.**
Farrar Straus and Giroux, an imprint of Macmillan
ISBN: 9780374318406

A child's perspective of growing up in post-World War II Romania is lovingly shared in this memoir. Each chapter is a beautiful vignette about Eva, a young girl, discovering her Jewish identity, her family's experiences during the war, and their dramatic journey to Israel.

Cry of the Giraffe by **Judie Oron.**
Annick Press
ISBN: 9781554512713

Wuditu, a young Ethiopian Jewish girl, and a group of fifteen family members set out on a dangerous journey on foot to reach a refugee camp in the Sudan with the hopes of being secretly airlifted to Israel. Based on a true story.

2010 Awards

Younger Readers

New Year at the Pier: A Rosh Hashanah Story by April Halprin Wayland.
Illustrations by Stéphane Jorisch.
Dial Books for Young Readers, an imprint of Penguin
ISBN: 9780803732797

The author employs her own memories of community *tashlich* at the beach in this loving, charmingly illustrated depiction of Izzy and his family and friends as they gently apologize for misdeeds, grant forgiveness, and toss breadcrumbs into the sea as part of their Rosh Hashanah observance.

Older Readers

The Importance of Wings by **Robin Friedman.**
Charlesbridge Publishing,
ISBN: 978158893305

The title of this coming-of-age novel refers to both the layered hairstyle Roxanne wants but cannot achieve with her straight locks, and what happens when an Israeli teen who wants to be more American discovers her inner beauty and self-confidence with the help of a friend.

Teen Readers

Tropical Secrets: Holocaust Refugees in Cuba by **Margarita Engle.**
Henry Holt Books for Young Readers, an imprint of Macmillan Children's Publishing Group
ISBN: 9780805089363

Newbery Honor Winner Engle continues to illuminate the lesser known history of Cuba -- the challenge of German refugees seeking a new home after Kristallnacht. Free verse in the voices of a German boy, a Cuban girl, and a Russian immigrant paint different perspectives of a complicated political and historical era.

Honor Books

Younger Readers

Nachshon, Who Was Afraid to Swim: A Passover Story by Deborah Bodin Cohen.
Illustrations by Jago.
Kar-Ben Publishing
ISBN: 9780822587651

Nachshon is not afraid of anything, except swimming. As the Jews leave Egypt, he realizes that in order to reach freedom he must face his fears and step into the water of the Red Sea. Imaginative artwork complements this story based on the Midrash.

Benjamin and the Silver Goblet by Jacqueline Jules.
Illustrations by Natascia Ugliano.
Kar-Ben Publishing
ISBN: 9780822587583

Benjamin the youngest of Jacob's sons, must accompany his brothers to Egypt and meet the governor (Joseph). This young boy's perspective of events remains true to the biblical narration while making it accessible to younger readers.

Yankee at the Seder by Elka Weber.
Illustrations by Adam Gustavson.
Tricycle Press
ISBN: 9781582462561

Based on a true tale, this beautifully illustrated story recounts the participation of a "Yankee Jew," Myer Levy, as a guest at a Virginia Passover Seder shortly after the end of the Civil War. Ten-year-old Jacob sees the words of the Haggadah ring true, as all who are hungry are welcome at the table.

You Never Heard of Sandy Koufax? by Jonah Winter
Illustrations by André Carrilho.
Schwartz & Wade Books, an imprint of Random House Children's Books
ISBN: 9780375837388

Koufax's rise from a Jewish boy in Brooklyn to one of the all-time greats of baseball as a Los Angeles Dodger is told in conversational style by an imagined teammate. A lenticular cover and magnificent artwork brings the left-hander's style to life.

Older Readers

Anne Frank: Her Life in Words and Pictures from the Archives of the Anne Frank House by **Menno Metselaar and Ruud van der Rol.**
Translated by Arnold J. Pomerans.
Roaring Brook Press, an imprint of Flash Point/Macmillan Children's Publishing Group
ISBN: 9781596435469

Archival photographs of Anne and her family, her actual writing and diary, and the annex are powerful and instrumental in bringing her life into context. The text details world events as well as Anne's life.

A Faraway Island by **Annika Thor.**
Translated by Linda Schenck.
Delacorte Books for Young Readers, an imprint of Random House Children's Books
ISBN: 9780385736176

Stephie and Ellie Steiner are sent from Vienna to Sweden to escape the Nazi threat, and must adjust to life on a small island off the mainland. Stephie comes of age as she meets the challenge of a new culture, a strict foster mother, and the worries about family in Austria.

Teen Readers

Lost by **Jacqueline Davies.**
Marshall Cavendish
ISBN: 9780761455356

The Triangle Shirtwaist Factory Fire provides the backdrop for this historical novel about friendship and loss.

Naomi's Song by **Selma Kritzer Silverberg.**
Jewish Publication Society
ISBN: 9780827608863

Following the biblical Book of Ruth Naomi's Song imagines the life experiences of Naomi, taking her from girlhood when she is orphaned to when Ruth marries and gives birth to Naomi's grandson.

Notable Books

Younger Readers

Where Is Grandpa Dennis? by Michelle Shapiro Abraham.
Illustrations by Janice Fried.
URJ Press
ISBN: 9780807410837

Gentle and wise, Devorah's mother (Grandpa Dennis' daughter) allows her to come up with her own answers and also helps her daughter feel a special closeness to her lost loved one by explaining some of the Jewish modes of remembrance.

Around the Shabbos Table by Seryl Berman.
Illustrations by Ari Binus.
Hachai Publishing
ISBN: 9781929628445

"In any seat, no matter where, in any spot, in any chair, whether it is here or there, I'll be happy anywhere!" is Tova Leiba's refrain as she gladly switches seats to accommodate her siblings.

The Secret Shofar of Barcelona by Jacqueline Dembar Greene.
Illustrations by Douglas Chyka.
Kar-Ben Publishing
ISBN: 9780822599449

A concert with "New World" instruments provides the opportunity for Conversos (hidden Jews) to blow the *shofar* on Rosh Hashanah.

Menorah under the Sea by Esther Susan Heller.
Photographs by David Ginsberg.
Kar-Ben Publishing
ISBN: 9780822573869

A beautifully photographed story shares the adventures of marine biologist David Ginsberg as he creates an underwater menorah out of starfish and sea urchins.

Today Is the Birthday of the World by Linda Heller.
Illustrations by Allison Jay.
Dutton Children's Books, an imprint of Penguin
ISBN: 9780525479055

Drawn from the liturgy of Rosh Hashanah, God is happy when his helpers are the best that they can be because "then the world is the best place that it can be, and there is no better birthday present."

The Waiting Wall by Leah Braunstein Levy.
Illustrations by Avi Katz.
Hachai Publishing
ISBN: 9781929628490

As two children visit the Western Wall in Jerusalem, they notice the details of their surroundings: the many steps to get there, the whiteness of the stone and its golden reflection of the sun, the shapes of the stones, and the special feeling of holiness that permeates this most holy site to Judaism. Amazing illustrations chronicle their path, providing both perspective and depth.

Sukkot Treasure Hunt by Allison Ofanansky.
Photographs by Eliyahu Alpern.
Kar-Ben Publishing
ISBN: 9780822587637

A family collects the four species needed to celebrate the Feast of Tabernacles in the area surrounding their home in Tsfat, Israel.

Fox Walked Alone by Barbara Reid.
Albert Whitman & Company
ISBN: 9780807525487

Fox follows the pairs of animals he sees, and eventually comes to Noah's Ark Plasticine is the medium used to create vibrant, three-dimensional art for this story in rhyme.

Older Readers

The Champion of Children: The Story of Janusz Korczak by Tomek Bogacki.
Frances Foster Books, an imprint of Farrar Straus and Giroux Books for Younger Readers/Macmillan
ISBN: 9780374341367

A warm, moral, true story, with beautiful illustrations, about a Holocaust hero -- Dr. Janusz Korczak -- who loved children and cared to Jewish orphans until they and he perished in the gas chambers

Guardian Angel House by Kathy Clark. (A Holocaust Remembrance Book for Young Readers).
Second Story Press
ISBN: 9781897187586

Based on the experiences of the author's mother and aunt, this fictionalized story of more than 100 girls hidden in a Budapest convent from 1944 until the liberation of Hungary emphasizes the relationships between the nuns and the Jewish children they sheltered.

Rebecca Series by Jacqueline Dembar Greene. (American Girl Collection). Illustrations by Robert Hunt.
American Girl
ISBN: Various

The latest historical character in the American Girl Collection lives on the Lower East Side in 1914, hopes to be an actress, and tries to balance an American way of life with traditional Jewish values.

Strawberry Hill by Mary Ann Hoberman.
Illustrations by Wendy Anderson Halperin.
Little Brown Books for Young Readers
ISBN: 9780316041362

When her family moves from New Haven to Stamford, Allie Sherman has to adjust to making new friends, juggle alliances, and handle the disappointment that her new street, Strawberry Hill, is not the bucolic, strawberry-laden lane she had envisioned.

The Mysteries of Beethoven's Hair by Russell Martin and Lydia Nibley.
Charlesbridge Publishing
ISBN: 9781570917141

There is considerable Jewish content in this excellent and highly readable account of Beethoven's life, the posthumous travels of a lock of his hair, and the search for clues to his illnesses via sophisticated scientific testing in the 20th century.

***The Man Who Flies with Birds* by Carol Garbuny Vogel and Yossi Leshem.**
Kar-Ben Publishing
ISBN: 9780822576433

Readers will learn about different kinds of birds, how they fly, and how the weather and wind affect their migration. Israeli ornithologist Leshem's work has encouraged cooperation between Israel and its Arab neighbors, and is helping with environmental concerns, which are recounted in a narrative accompanied by spectacular pictures of birds and clear maps and illustrations.

***Clay Man: The Golem of Prague* by Irene N. Watts.**
Illustrations by Kathryn E. Shoemaker.
Tundra Books
ISBN: 9780887768804

There are many legends of the man of mud created by Rabbi Yehudah Loew to help the Jews of Prague during the precarious times of the late 1500's. This retelling by the Maharal's imagined young son works well to illustrate the wonder at this strange and mighty creature.

***Elvina's Mirror* by Sylvie Weil.**
Jewish Publication Society
ISBN: 9780827608856

In this sequel to *Guardian Angel* (Scholastic, 2004), Elvina still talks to Mazal, her Guardian Angel, for help with two challenges: a family from German shunned by the community; and a handsome knight who befriends her. Rashi's granddaughter uses her thirst for knowledge and her compassion for others to handle both situations.

Teen Readers

***The Disappearing Dowry: An Ezra Melamed Mystery* by Libi Astaire.**
Zahav Press, a imprint of Targum
ISBN: 9781568715019

A mystery with Jewish practices and values embedded: the narrator, A Jewish girl in 1810 London, tells the "megillah" of her wealthy, observant family's plans for her sister Hannah's wedding, which are suddenly interrupted by the loss of the family fortune through bank failures and theft.

A Family Secret/The Search **by Eric Heuvel.**
Farrar Straus and Giroux Books for Younger Readers, an imprint of Macmillan
ISBN: 978037432271/9780374365172

The situation in the Netherlands during World War II is explored in these graphic novels. In *A Family Secret*, Helena tells her grandson Jeroen about her experiences during the German occupation and how she lost both her father and her best friend Esther at the hands of the Nazis. In *The Search*, Esther remembers her own experience during the Holocaust as a Jewish girl living in Amsterdam, and recounts to her grandson Daniel and his friend Jeroen how she survived by going into hiding in the countryside.

So Punk Rock (and Other Ways to Disappoint Your Mother) **by Micol Ostow.**
Illustrations by David Ostow.
Flux
ISBN: 9780738714714

The Ostows combine graphic novel vignettes filled with sarcastic commentary with a coming-of-age novel in which Ari Abramson is struggling to find his true calling and identity while also trying to fit in, hoping that playing in a band will win him popularity and the girl of his dreams.

Cursing Columbus **by Eve Tal.**
Cinco Puntos Press
ISBN: 9781933693590

Told in the duel voices of Raizel and Lemmel in alternating chapters and scenarios, Tal crafts a realistic and poignant picture of an immigrant family's struggles in the early 20th century in this sequel to *Double Crossing* (2005).

Puppet **by Eva Wiseman.**
Tundra Books
ISBN: 9780887768286

A servant girl disappears from her Hungarian village in the sprint of 1882, and the Jews of the community are blamed in this fictionalized account of "the last blood libel trial in Europe." Narrated b Julie, another servant girl with her own challenges, the ills of religious superstition, prejudice, and false accusations come to bear in this emotionally charged novel.

The Other Half of Life **by Kim Ablon Whitney.**
Alfred A. Knopf, an imprint of Random House
ISBN: 9780375852190

Thomas, a fifteen-year-old boy forced to leave his parents in Nazi Germany, experiences many emotions aboard a ship destined for Cuba. This historical fiction is based on the story of the MS St. Louis.

All Ages

JPS Illustrated Children's Bible by **Ellen Frankel.**
Illustrations by Avi Katz.
Jewish Publication Society
ISBN: 9780827608917

Fifty-three uniquely chosen Bible legends capture the language and cadence of the Hebrew bible. Frankel succeeds in creating an age-appropriate interpretation of the most intriguing and familiar stories that allow families to glean the essence of Jewish teachings, ethics, and history.

2009 Awards

Younger Readers

As Good As Anybody: Martin Luther King, Jr. and Abraham Joshua Heschel's Amazing March toward Freedom by **Richard Michelson.**
Illustrations by Raúl Colón.
Alfred A. Knopf, an imprint of Random House Children's Books
ISBN: 9780375833359

This fictionalized parallel biography of Reverend Martin Luther King, Jr. and Rabbi Abraham Joshua Heschel, presents a beautiful and inspiring tribute to a little known alliance in American history. Colón's stunning illustrations with subtle coloring bring the text, and the message of persistence, justice, and brotherhood, to life.

Older Readers

Brooklyn Bridge by **Karen Hesse.**
Feiwel & Friends, an imprint of Macmillan
ISBN: 9780312378868

While his family left the anti-Semitism of Russia to build the American dream, Joey Michtom's dream is to visit the glittering Coney Island. Crafting a story from the spark of a true event, the invention of the Teddy Bear in 1903, Hesse masterfully weaves multiple themes of hard-work, survival, homelessness, and familial dedication.

Teen Readers

A Bottle in the Gaza Sea **by Valerie Zenatti.**
Bloomsbury
ISBN: 9781599902005

This honest yet hopeful story about the relationship between an Israeli girl and a Palestinian boy via e-mail and instant messaging conveys the confusion, anger, exhaustion, and depression felt by many young people during the 2003 Intifada.

Honor Books

Younger Readers

Engineer Ari and the Rosh Hashanah Ride **by Deborah Bodin Cohen.**
Illustrations by Shahar Kober.
Kar-Ben Publishing
ISBN: 9780822586487

Ari is selected to engineer the first train between Jaffa and Jerusalem. Filled with pride, he boasts to his friends and neglects to say good-bye before he sets off. As the train stops to collect the necessary items to celebrate the Jewish New Year, Ari is reminded of the true meaning of the holiday. Charming, colorful illustrations give the reader a sense of what Israel's countryside might have looked like in 1892.

Sarah Laughs **by Jacqueline Jules.**
Illustrations by Natascia Ugliano.
Kar-Ben Publishing
ISBN: 9780822599340

The story of Sarah, the biblical matriarch, is told beginning with her childhood in Ur and continuing through her marriage to Abraham, their journey to Canaan, and the eventual birth of Isaac. Vibrant illustrations show her sweet, generous and loving personality, as well as the starry nights and windswept deserts on the way to Canaan.

A is for Abraham: A Jewish Family Alphabet by Richard Michelson.
Illustrations by Ron Mazellan.
Sleeping Bear Press
ISBN: 9781585363223

From A for Abraham to Z for Zayde, this alphabet book, illustrated by fluid, realistic paintings, provides a wealth of information about Jewish culture, history, personalities, holidays, customs, and ceremonies.

Naming Liberty by Jane Yolen.
Illustrations by Jim Burke.
Philomel Books, an imprint of Penguin
ISBN: 9780399242502

Parallel stories tell the arrival of two young ladies to the United States - Gitl, the daughter of a Russian family, who decide to emigrate to avoid the pogroms and persecution of Czarist Russia and the Statue of Liberty, conceived and developed by the young French artist Frederic Auguste Bartholdi as a commemoration for America's centennial birthday. Illustrations in counterpart oil paint panels reflect the 19th century Eastern European village against the more modern cities of Paris and New York.

Older Readers

Memories of Babi by Aranka Siegal.
Farrar Straus and Giroux
ISBN: 9780374399788

Eight short episodic stories reflect the author's childhood in a small village in Hungary and incorporate Jewish values of kindness, generosity, honesty, help for the less fortunate, and special moments filled with a little adventure, amusing escapades, and lots of love.

Teen Readers

Freefall by Anna Levine.
Greenwillow Books, an imprint of HarperCollins
ISBN: 9780061576546

Aggie Jacobs, a typical eighteen-year-old Israeli girl, decides to try out for an elite female combat unit in the Israeli army. Realistic dialogue and a first person narrative provide a genuine look at the realities of Israeli military life through the eyes of a young woman.

Notable Books
Younger Readers

Mysterious Guests: A Sukkot Story by Eric Kimmel.
Illustrations by Katya Krenina.
Holiday House
ISBN: 9780823418930

During the festival of Sukkot, Eben builds a fancy sukkah but he makes the poor stand in the corner and eat leftovers. His brother Ezra's sukkah is plain, but he welcomes all who come with a full heart. When the *ushpizin* visit they bestow an identical blessing -- may this sukkah's outside be like its inside -- with very different results.

Jodie's Hanukkah Dig by Anna Levine.
Illustrations by Knesia Topaz.
Kar-Ben Publsihing
ISBN: 9780822573913

Jodie wants to be an archaeologist in Israeli like her father. When they visit a dig in Modi'in, she finds a way to help out and makes an important discovery related to the history of Hanukkah.

Harvest of Light by Allison Ofanansky.
Photographs by Eliyahu Alpern.
Kar-Ben Publishing
ISBN: 9780822573890

From the first spring blossoms to the harvesting of green olives before Sukkot, an Israeli family works together throughout the year, culminating in the celebration of Hanukkah with flickering wicks floating in the precious oil they have produced together.

Sammy Spider's First Shavuot by Sylvia Rouss.
Illustrations by Katherine Janus Kahn.
Kar-Ben Publishing
ISBN: 9780822572244

Continuing the popular series, Sammy Spider learns about Shavuot, first with the traditional blintz and fruit recipes, then with the holiday's significance, and finally with a little experimentation of his own.

My Tzitzis Book by Elisheva Schreiber.
Illustrations by Batsheva Ravad.
Translated by Sherie Gross.
Feldheim
ISBN: 9781598261154

This informative explanation of the meaning of wearing a four-cornered garment with *tzitzis* is augmented with creative clay figures of scenes of boys and men wearing their *tallis katan* beneath their everyday clothing.

Hanukkah Haiku by Harriet Ziefert.
Illustrations by Karla Gudeon.
Blue Apple Books
ISBN: 9781934706336

Eight haikus reflect on specific aspects of the Hanukkah such as candle lighting, dreidel spinning, and latke frying. The simply poetry is embellished with rich and deeply colored paintings and graduated paper size is used to uncover each new candle.

Older Readers

The Boy Who Dared: A Novel Based on the True Story of a Hitler Youth by **Susan Campbell Bartoletti.**
Scholastic
ISBN: 9780439680134

A powerful work of historical fiction portraying key moments in the life of a real German teenager during World War II. As he waits in prison, Helmuth Hubener reflects on events that led to the day of his execution for the crimes of listening to foreign newscasts, creating and distributing pamphlets, and for his resistance to the Nazi Party.

The Walls of Cartegena by Julie Durango.
Illustrations by Tom Pohrt.
Simon & Schuster Books for Young Readers
ISBN: 9781416941026

Because of his intelligence and facility with languages, thirteen-year-old Calepino escapes the usual fate of slaves delivered by ship from Africa to Cartagena (Columbia), and grows up to become a protégé of a kind Jesuit priest, an interpreter, and a helper in the leper colony where he befriends a Jewish doctor, a convert to Christianity.

Capturing the Moon by Edward Feinstein.
Behrman House
ISBN: 9780874418408

Each story in this collection includes a short description of the value presented and follow-up discussion questions. Stories are grouped into six categories: "What Really Matters in Life?" "Doing What's Right," "It's Up to You," "Teachers and Friends," "Hidden Truths," and "The Miracle of Jewish Life."

Kristallnacht, the Night of Broken Glass: Igniting the Nazi War against Jews by Stephanie Fitzgerald.
Compass Point Books
ISBN: 9780756534899

Created for school research, this well-designed book includes clear, accurate information, historic photographs with informative captions, a glossary, bibliography, source notes, and timeline. Personal reflections and memories by eyewitnesses add to the impact of the account, which directly confronts Nazi lies about the Jews.

My Chocolate Year by Charlotte Herman.
Illustrations by LeUyen Pham.
Simon & Schuster Books for Younger Readers
ISBN: 9781416933410

Fifth grader Dorrie Meyers embarks on an exciting school year with a favorite teacher and the Sweet Semester dessert and essay contest. World War II has just ended, and when her cousin Victor, the sole Holocaust survivor of the family come to live with her family, he shares a recipe from his family's bakery to help her with the contest.

The Mozart Question by Michael Morpurgo.
Illustrations by Michael Forman.
Candlewick Press
ISBN: 1406306484

Paolo Levi, a fictional Italian violin prodigy, tells the secret tale of his parents' experience as musicians in a concentration camp orchestra.

Boys of Steel: The Creators of Superman by Marc Tyler Nobleman.
Illustrations by Ross McDonald.
Alfred A. Knopf, an imprint of Random House
ISBN: 9780375838026

A picture book biography of Jerry Siegel and Joe Shuster , two shy, nerdy, bespectacled Jewish teens from Cleveland, who succeed in creating an American icon of bravery, super strength, and altruistic invincibility.

The Bat-Chen Diaries: Selected Writings by Bat-Chen Shahak.
Kar-Ben Publishing
ISBN: 9780822588078

This is the published diary, including poems, letters, and eulogies, of an Israeli girl who was murdered by a suicide bomber in Tel Aviv's Disengoff Center at Purim on her fifteenth birthday.

Keeping Israel Safe: Serving in the Israel Defense Forces by Barbara Sofer.
Kar-Ben Publishing
ISBN: 9780822572213

Four different experiences told through the voices of individual Israeli teenagers, two girls and two boys, preparing to enter Israeli military service recount the history and many levels and opportunities available for youth reaching the required draft age.

Honey Cake by Joan Betty Stuchner.
Illustrations by Cynthia Nugent.
Stepping Stone, an imprint of Random House
ISBN: 9780675851896

This easy chapter book gently introduces readers to World War II and the Danish resistance through the story of ten-year-old David, who lives in Copenhagen during the German occupation.

Teen Readers

Nothing by **Robin Friedman.**
Flux
ISBN: 9780738713045

In alternating chapters, Parker Rabinowitz and his younger sister Danielle gradually reveal the terrible secret -- a serious eating disorder -- that hides behind Parker's good looks, great grades, ambitious college resume, pre-med plans, and success with girls.

Rutka's Notebook: A Voice from the Holocaust by **Rutka Laskier.**
Time, Inc. Home Entertainment
ISBN: 9781603200196

A Jewish girl's diary, describing her life in the days before her family was sent to Auschwitz, was hidden under Polish floorboards in 1943, retrieved in 1945, and miraculously rediscovered in 2006, allowing Zahava Laskier Scherz to explore the brief life of the half-sister she never knew.

Gravity by **Leanne Lieberman.**
Orca Book Publishers
ISBN: 9781554690497
When Elisheva, a nature-loving sophomore in an all-girls Jewish high school, feels a sexual attraction to Lindsay, a girl she meets during a summer by the lake, all of her Orthodox upbringing and observances come into question.

The Freak by **Carol Matas.**
Key Porter Books
ISBN: 9781552639304

When fifteen-year-old Jade awakens from a life-threatening illness and finds she can see the future, her life takes some very strange turns. This is the first book in a series, which continues with *Visions* and *Far*.

All Ages

Genesis -- The Book with Seventy Faces: a Guide for the Family by **Esther Takac.**
Illustrations by Anna Pignataro.
Pitspopany Press
ISBN: 9781932687927

This beautifully designed guide, filled with watercolor, pen and ink, and crayon drawings illuminates the twelve *parshiot* of the book of Genesis and provides a wonderful resource to learn, study, and interpret from the perspective of the sages, modern scholars, *Midrash*, legends, and kabbalah.

Celebrating with Jewish Crafts by Rebecca Edid Ruzansky.
Photographs by Roberto Zeballos-Peralta.
Rebecca Edid Ruzansky
ISBN: 9780615171142

Crafts for Rosh Hashanah, Yom Kippur, Sukkot, Shmini Atzeret and Simchat Torah, Hanukkah, Purim, Passover, and Shavuot are presented with explicit instructions, clear color photographs and tips on techniques and supplies. A Jewish crafter's dream!

2008 Awards

Younger Readers
The Bedtime Sh'ma by Sarah Gershman.
Illustrations by Kristina Swarner.
EKS Publishing
ISBN: 0939144557

With accessible language, this book helps young children understand the meaning and concepts of the Sh'ma prayers. A CD is included creating a soft sound for falling asleep or learning the Hebrew of the nighttime prayers.

Older Readers

The Entertainer and the Dybbuk by Sid Fleischman.
HarperCollins Children's Books
ISBN: 0061344451

When the spirit of a 12-year old Jewish boy, murdered by the Nazis possesses the body of an American GI traveling through Europe as a second-rate ventriloquist, the pair is able to unmask the Nazi responsible.

Teen Readers

Strange Relations by Sonia Levitin.
Knopf, an imprint of Random House Children's Books
ISBN: 0375837515

Fifteen-year-old Marne decides to spend the summer with her Aunt Carole in Hawaii. But, Aunt Carole is now Aunt Chaya, married to a Chabad Rabbi with seven children. What Marne anticipates will be a relaxing summer of jogging on the beach, surfing, sun tanning, and shopping turns out to be a summer of exploration, spirituality, and growth.

Honor Books
Younger Readers

The Castle on Hester Street by Linda Heller.
Illustrations by Boris Kulikov.
Simon & Schuster
ISBN: 0689874340

A young girl visiting her grandparents learns the story of their immigration to the United States, their life on the Lower East Side of New York City, and how they met in this newly illustrated edition, winner of the Sydney Taylor Book Award when it was first released in 1982.

Letter on the Wind: A Chanukah Tale by Sarah Marwil Lamstein.
Illustrations by Neil Waldman.
Boyds Mills Press
ISBN: 1932425748

When his village suffers a drought and there will be no olives oil for the Chanukah menorahs, Hayim, a poor and humble man, writes a letter to the Almighty to request enough oil for the entire village.

Light by Jane Breskin Zalben.
Dutton Children's Books, an imprint of Penguin Young Readers Group
ISBN: 0525478272

The concepts of *tikkun olam* and making the world a better place are explained simply yet lyrically in this gorgeously illustrated volume inspired by a 16th-century Midrash.

Older Readers

Holocaust: The Events and Their Impact on Real People by Angela Gluck Wood and Dan Stone.
DK Publishing
ISBN: 0756625351

This comprehensive, readable, impressively visual history of the Holocaust ranges across the years from the origins of Jews, life in Europe, and the history of anti-Semitism to the post-war period, including the survivors, Nazi trials, stolen property, and concentration camps and present-day memorials. The book is supplemented by a DVD of personal testimonies from the archive of the USC Shoah Foundation Institute for Visual History and Education.

The Secret of Priest's Grotto: A Holocaust Survival Story by Peter Lane Taylor and Christos Nicola.
Kar-Ben Publishing
ISBN: 1580132618

The amazing story of how a group of thirty-eight Jews managed to survive during World War II for nearly a year in the underground caves of the Western Ukraine is told with captivating narratives and descriptions, sharp full-color photographs, and an attractive lay-out and design.

Teen Readers

Let Sleeping Dogs Lie by Mirjam Pressler.
Translated by Erik J. Macki.
Front Street
ISBN: 1932425845

Seventeen year-old Johanna Riemenschneider's idyllic, privileged childhood comes to an abrupt end when she travels to Israel with her German classmates to meet Jewish alumni of their high school who fled the town during World War II.

Notable Books

Younger Readers

My Cousin Tamar Lives in Israel by Michelle Shapiro Abraham.
Illustrations by Ann D. Koffsky.
URJ
ISBN: 0807409898

A young North American boy compares his observances of the Jewish holidays to those of his cousin Tamar who lives in Israel.

***A Nickel, a Trolley, a Treasure House* by Sharon Reiss Baker.**
Illustrations by Beth Peck.
Viking   Children's Books, an imprint of Penguin
ISBN: 9780670059829

Young Lionel loves to draw, a hobby not much appreciated by his immigrantparents. When his teacher sees his drawings, she arranges to take him, by trolley, to the Metropolitan Museum of Art.

***Shuli and Me: From Slavery to Freedom* by Joan Benjamin-Farren.**
Black Jasmine
ISBN: 097888020X
Accompanied by the text for counting the Omer in Hebrew and English, a young girl narrates what happens to the Children of Israel from their first Passover until the giving of the Torah at Mount Sinai.

***Papa Jethro* by Deborah Bodin Cohen.**
Illustrations by Jane Dippold.
Kar-Ben Publishing
 ISBN: 9781580135803

A young girl asks her grandfather why she goes to synagogue and he goes to church. He explains that she is Jewish and he is Christian and retells the biblical story of Jethro, the Midianite father-in-law of Moses.

***Hanukkah Moon* by Deborah da Costa.**
Illustrations by Gosia Mosz.
Kar-Ben Publishing
ISBN: 9781580132442

Isobel spends the first three nights of Hanukkah with her Aunt Luisa, who has just emigrated from Mexico. She learns how to take pictures with her new camera, creates a bird scrapbook, bakes dreidel-shaped cookies while singing "I Have a Little Dreidel" in English and Spanish, and observes Rosh Chodesh, the celebration of the new moon.

***Celebrate Passover with Matzah, Maror and Memories* by Deborah Heiligman (Holidays Around the World).**
National Geographic
ISBN: 9781426300189

Celebrate Rosh Hashanah & Yom Kippur with Honey, Prayers, and the Shofar by **Deborah Heiligman (Holidays Around the World).**
National Geographic
ISBN: 9781426300769

Full-color photographs and an attractive layout combine with an informative text to create a wonderful introduction to the Jewish holidays of Passover, Rosh Hashanah and Yom Kippur. The photographs include contemporary Jews in the United States, Peru, Portugal, Morocco, Ukraine, Thailand, Israel, Zimbabwe, Yemen, Uganda, and China.

Five Little Gefiltes by **Dave Horowitz.**
G.P. Putnam's Sons, an imprint of Penguin
ISBN: 9780399246081

Instead of ducklings, it's five little gefilte fish balls wearing black bowler hats who daily wander away from their worried mother as they set out to see the sights of New York.

Mendel's Accordion by **Heidi Smith Hyde.**
Illustrations by Johanna van der Sterre.
Kar-Ben Publishing
ISBN: 9781580132121
Mendel plays the accordion in his small village, but when things become difficult for the Jews of Eastern Europe, Mendel takes his accordion to America. When his great-grandson discovers the old accordion in the attic, he repairs it and pledges to learn to play.

Abraham's Search for God by **Jacqueline Jules.**
Illustrations by Natascia Ugliano.
Kar-Ben Publishing
ISBN: 978580132435

Based on *midrashim*, this is the story of how Abraham came to believe in only one God when everyone around him worshipped idols.

A Mezuzah on the Door by **Amy Meltzer.**
Illustrations by Janice Fried.
Kar-Ben Publishing
ISBN: 9781580132497

When Noah's family moves from an apartment in the city to a house in the suburbs, his family plans a *Hanukkat Habayit* party to put up the *mezuzot* and celebrate their new home.

Ten Good Rules: A Counting Book by Susan Remick Topek.
Photographs by Tod Cohen.
Kar-Ben Publishing
ISBN: 9781580132091

With the same simple, child-friendly text as the original 1991 edition, this new version features full-color photographs of contemporary children illustrating the Ten Commandments.

Older Readers

Out of Line: Growing Up Soviet by **Tina Grimberg.**
Tundra Books
ISBN: 9780887768033
Tina Grimberg's memoir of growing up in the Soviet Union in the 1960's and 1970's provides the detailed descriptions of family, school and home that bring history to life.

A Picture for Marc by **Eric A. Kimmel.**
Illustrations by Matthew Trueman.
Random House Children's Books
ISBN: 9780375832536

Very loosely based on the life of Marc Chagall, this highly fictionalized, light-hearted biography focuses on the beginning of the artist's experience with drawing.

Anne Frank: The Young Writer Who Told the World Her Story by **Ann Kramer (World History Biographies).**
National Geographic
ISBN: 9781426300042

Presented in simple language and enhanced by a wealth of photos, maps, timelines, and information boxes, this well-designed book nicely combines the Frank family's experiences with events in Europe before and during World War II.

The Silver Cup by **Constance Leeds.**
Viking Children's Books, an imprint of Penguin
ISBN: 9780670061570

The Crusades, as well as the superstitions and bleakness of Germany in 1096, are the backdrop for the story of Anna, a young girl who befriends Leah, the lone Jewish survivor of the massacre of the Worms Ghetto.

Passover around the World by Tami Lehman-Wilzig.
Illustrations by Elizabeth Wolf.
Kar-Ben Publishing
ISBN: 1580132138

The customs and observances of Passover are described in this colorful book that includes stories, recipes, and a brief history and description of the Jewish communities of the United States, Gibraltar, Turkey, Ethiopia, India, Israel, Iran, and Morocco.

Whirlwind by Carol Matas.
Orca Book Publishers
ISBN: 9781551437033

Fifteen-year-old Ben immigrates to Seattle in 1942 with his family. He quickly befriends John, a Japanese-American classmate, as both boys endure taunting from their peers because of their origins.

Penina Levine Is a Hard-Boiled Egg by Rebecca O'Connell.
Illustrations by Majella Lue Sue.
Roaring Brook Press
ISBN: 9781596431409

Penina Levine is one of only two Jewish children in her sixth grade class. When her teacher gives the class an assignment -- writing a letter as the Easter Bunny -- Penina balks. Is she standing up for a meaningful principle, or is it okay to willingly participate in someone else's culture?

All-Star Season by T.S. Yavin.
Kar-Ben Publishing
ISBN: 978580132114

Brothers Reuven and Avi are the best pitcher and catcher duo in the league. But, when only one player from each team makes the All-Stars, which brother will be selected?

Teen Readers

How to Ruin My Teenage Life by **Simone Elkeles.**
Flux
ISBN: 9780738710198

Continuing her adventures from *How to Ruin a Summer Vacation*, Amy Nelson-Barak is now living with her Israeli father in Chicago and spending her senior year at the Chicago Academy while she waits for the summer so she can return to Israel to see her family and her "non-boyfriend" Avi again.

Cures for Heartbreak by **Margo Rabb.**
Delacorte Press an imprint of Random House
ISBN: 9780385734028

Mia Pearlman's mother dies just days after being diagnosed with melanoma, leaving Mia, her older sister Alex, and her father bereft. Mia and Alex's lives become further complicated when their father has a heart attack only month later. A poignant and insightful study of grief and life in one Jewish family.

Hidden on the Mountain: Stories of Children Sheltered from the Nazis in Le Chambon by **Deborah Durlan DeSaix and Karen Gray Ruelle.**
Holiday House
ISBN: 9780823419289

A small, Protestant town in the plateau region of South Central France became an example of faith and courage during World War II when the citizens sheltered thousands of refugees, most of them Jewish, and protected them from the Nazis.

Homeland: The Illustrated History of the State of Israel by **Marv Wolfman. Illustrations by Mario Ruiz.**
Nachshon Press
ISBN: 9780977150717

This over-sized graphic non-fiction volume begins with Biblical Israel, proceeds through Jewish history, the creation of the modern state of Israel, the wars, the Intifada, Arab terrorism, efforts toward peace, and includes the broad contemporary accomplishments of Israelis in various fields.

2007 Awards

Younger Readers

Hanukkah at Valley Forge by Stephen Krensky.
Illustrations by Greg Harlin.
Dutton Children's Books
ISBN: 0525477381

During the grim winter at Valley Forge, a Polish-born soldier tells General Washington about Hanukkah, who draws a parallel between the Macabbee's war against their foes with the American war against the British oppressors. Beautiful watercolor illustrations add immeasurably to a delightful and inspirational account of this legendary encounter.

Older Readers

Julia's Kitchen by Brenda A. Ferber.
Farrar Straus and Giroux
ISBN: 0374399328

When Cara Segal loses her mother and younger sister in a house fire, she questions her belief in God, struggles with her relationship with her father, and tries to find ways to hold onto the memories of her family in this deeply moving novel that will touch the hearts of all readers.

Teen Readers

The Book Thief by Markus Zusak.
Alfred A. Knopf, an imprint of Random House
ISBN: 0375831002

Death narrates the story of Leisl Meminger, a Lutheran girl in Nazi Germany who sustains herself and those close to her with her love of books and reading. An engaging story that resonates with the full spectrum of human emotions and experiences.

Honor Books
Younger Readers

The White Ram: A Story of Abraham and Isaac by **Mordicai Gerstein.**
Holiday House
ISBN: 0823418979

This beautifully illustrated book adds another dimension to the biblical account of when God commanded Abraham to sacrifice Isaac. Although "the Evil One" seeks to deter him from his mission, the ram is able to complete it, and his sacrifice provides a rich inheritance for the Jewish people, including the foundations of Jerusalem, and the strings of David's harp.

I Am Marc Chagall by **Bimba Landmann.**
Eerdmans Books for Young Readers
ISBN 0802853056

With text loosely based on Marc Chagall's autobiography, this picture book features detailed, intricate three-dimensional mixed media illustrations that are a collage of fabrics, metals, woods, papers, clay, photographs, and objects from nature.

Shlemazel and the Remarkable Spoon of Pohost by **Ann Redisch Stampler.**
Illustrations by Jacqueline M. Cohen.
Clarion Books
ISBN 0618369597

Bright, colorful, animated illustrations enhance this delightfully entertaining story of Shlemazel who is so convinced that he is the most unlucky person in the world that he is afraid to get off his front porch. But when he believes that he has the amazing, remarkable spoon of Pohost, Shlemazel learns the pleasure of a good day's work, finds a wife, and discovers that he doesn't need luck to be happy.

Rebecca's Journey Home by **Brynn Olenberg Sugarman.**
Illustrations by Michelle Shapiro.
Kar-Ben Publishing
ISBN: 15801315 73

The story of a Jewish-American family who adopts a child from Vietnam is recounted with warmth and sensitivity from the adoption procedure and the trip to Asia to the baby's first Shabbat with her new family and her conversion and naming ceremony.

Older Readers

Vive La Paris by **Esme Raji Codell.**
Hyperion Books for Children
ISBN: 0786851244

Fifth-grader Paris McCray reveals what she has discovered about life in the process of taking piano lessons from Mrs. Rosen, a Holocaust. survivor with a sense of humor.

Solomon and the Ant and Other Jewish Folktales by **Sheldon Oberman.**
Introduction and Commentary by Peninnah Schram.
Boyds Mills Press
ISBN 1590783077

From simple stories, to valuable lessons, to an idea of what life was like in Rambam's time or how a holiday was celebrated in Russia, these folktales are brilliant in their simplicity. They can be read straight through, compared and contrasted, embellished upon, or edited for educational purposes. (

Yellow Star by **Jennifer Roy.**
Marshall Cavendish
ISBN 076145277X

Told in verse, this is the story of Syvia Perlmutter, one of twelve surviving children, who hid in the Lodz Ghetto with her family.

The Night of the Burning: Devorah's Story by **Linda Press Wulf.**
Farrar Straus and Giroux
ISBN: 0374364192

This first-person narrative is an insightful exploration of the effects of traumatic experiences, and an ultimately hopeful portrait of a young Jewish girl who survives a brutal pogrom in Russia, and journeys to an orphanage and a new life in South Africa.

Teen Readers

Incantation by Alice Hoffman.
Little, Brown and Company
ISBN 0316010197

Amidst book burnings, trials, and murders, sixteen-year-old Estrella DeMadrigal, living in Spain in 1500, learns that her family is part of a secret community of Jews who converted to Catholicism to avoid persecution.

A Brief Chapter in My Impossible Life by Dana Reinhardt.
Wendy Lamb Books, an imprint of Random House
ISBN: 0385746989

In this poignant story, Simone Turner meets Rivka, her biological mother, and learns about the circumstances of her adoption – how Rivka, a Hasidic Jew, became pregnant at sixteen and was shunned by her family, became a photographer and moved to Cape Cod, and now suffers from terminal cancer.

Notable Books
Younger Readers

I Have a Little Dreidel by Maxie Baum.
Illustrations by Julie Paschkis.
Scholastic
ISBN: 0439649978

The familiar dreidel song is embellished with new verses detailing a contemporary family's celebration of Hanukkah. Besides playing dreidel, the family makes potato latkes, lights the menorah, and enjoys a delicious dinner together.

Gershwin's Rhapsody in Blue by Anna Harwell Celenza.
Illustrations by JoAnn E. Kitchel.
Charlesbridge
ISBN: 1570915563

A fictionalized account of the creation of George Gershwin's "Rhapsody in Blue" details how the composer was inspired b the rhythm of a train ride, the klezmer band at his brother's Bar Mitzvah, and the harmonies of nightclub dance music, ragtime and the blues.

Eight Wild Nights: A Family Hanukkah Tale by Brian P. Cleary. Illustrations by David Udovic.
Kar-Ben Publishing
ISBN: 1580131522

This rhyming story depicts a family celebration that includes: cleaning the house, inviting friends and neighbors, spills, a new method of winning *gelt*, the miracle of toilet paper, a broken VCR, a scary side dish, presents that were not on the wish list, donuts, singing, and finally quiet and calm.

On Sukkot and Simchat Torah by Cathy Goldberg Fishman. Illustrations by Melanie Hall.
Kar-Ben Publishing
ISBN: 1580131654

A young girl narrates her family's celebration of Sukkot and Simchat Torah: building an decorating the sukkah, inviting the *ushpizin*, eating and sitting in the sukkah, blessing the *lulav* and *etrog*, going to the synagogue for Shemini Atzeret, marching and dancing on Simchat Torah, and listening to her mother chant from the Torah.

With All Your Heart: A Shabbatand Festival Companion edited by Rabbi Julie K. Gordon
Minneapolis Jewish Day School
ISBN: 1580132634

With adorable color illustrations by students and Hebrew, English and transliterations for all of the prayers and readings, this is a great resource for families and schools and will encourage all levels of participation in the Jewish holidays and Shabbat.

Celebrate Hanukkah with Light, Lakes and Dreidels by Deborah Heiligman (Holidays around the World).
National Geographic
ISBN: 0792259246

Full-color photographs from Israel, India, Peru, Uganda, Poland, Los Angeles, Ghana, and Rome combine with an interesting, informative text to create a stunning introduction to Hanukkah focusing on light, Jewish identity, freedom, and the celebration of miracles.

Much, Much Better by Chaim Kosofsky.
Illustrations by Jessica Schiffman.
Hachai Publishing
ISBN: 1929628226

Each week Shlomo and Miriam tidy up their house and prepare for Shabbat. When a strange guest visits, he is so appreciative of their hospitality that he offers them a blessing. It is not until Shlomo and Miriam welcome the birth of their baby boy that they fully understand the visitor's blessing and his true identity as Elijah the Prophet.

It's Shofar Time! by Latifa Berry Kropf.
Photographs by Tod Cohen.
Kar-Ben Publishing
ISBN: 1580131581

In this installment of the photo essay series by Kropf and Cohen, children blow the shofar, create New Year's cards, bake round challah, dip apples in honey, see the Torah dressed in white, and perform *tashlich*. Instructions for making a shofar craft project are included along with a brief note about Rosh Hashanah.

Willy & Max: A Holocaust Story by Amy Littlesugar.
Illustrations by William Low.
Philomel Books
ISBN: 0399234837

This heartwarming tale of kindness, truth, honesty, and friendship during the Holocaust also introduces readers to the widespread theft and looting by the Nazis of artwork belonging to European Jews.

Hammerin' Hank: The Life of Hank Greenberg by Yona Zeldis McDonough.
Illustrations by Malcah Zeldis.
Walker & Company
ISBN: 0802789978

This picture book biography details Hank Greenberg's childhood and his college basketball and professional baseball career, as well as the anti-Semitism that he faced from frans and players and his encounter with Jackie Robinson.

Across the Alley by Richard Michelson.
Illustrations by E. B. Lewis.
G.P. Putnam's Sons
ISBN: 0399239707

Willie, an African-American, and Abe, a Jew, become friends as they look out their bedroom windows in post-World War II Brooklyn, New York. They form a unique bond and bash stereotype as Abe plays baseball and Willie gives a violin concert in the synagogue.

A Grandma Like Yours/A Grandpa Like Yours by Andria Warmflash **Rosenbaum.**
Illustrations by Barb Bjornson.
Kar-Ben Publishing
ISBN: 1580131674

In this two-in-one "flip book," animal grandmothers and grandfathers have great fun with their grandchildren baking challah, delivering Purim treats, planting trees for Tu B'Shvat, and making matzah.

The Little, Little House by Jessica Souhami.
Frances Lincoln Limited
ISBN: 1845071085

Joseph can no longer tolerate being "jammed and crammed, so squashed and squeezed," so he goes to Aunty Bella, who suggests he brings the chickens, rooster, cow and goat into the house. When she finally tells him to put the animals back in the yard, Joseph and his family enjoy the quiet and spaciousness of their house at a Shabbat meal.

Older Readers

The Secret World of Kabbalah by Judith Z. Abrams.
Kar-Ben Publishing
ISBN: 15801322403

Short chapters, text boxes, illustrations and diagrams dissect the complicated subject matter of Kabbalah, mysticism, Kabbalistic texts and more in this highly readable, succinct and fascinating introduction.

Escape! The Story of the Great Houdini by Sid Fleischman.
Greenwillow Books
ISBN: 0060850949

Full of colorful language, this biography of Houdini is infused with the showman's Jewish side, recalling his birth as Ehrich Weiss to an impoverished but scholarly rabbi in a Budapest ghetto, his self-invention and brashness as an immigrant., the effects of anti-Semitism, and his lifelong love of learning.

Escaping into the Night by D. Dina Friedman.
Simon & Schuster Books for Young Readers
ISBN: 1416902589

When her mother and others do not come back from work, Halina is forced to deal with her absence and escape from the ghetto to save her own life. She joins the partisans in the woods, and survives World War II by using her wits and inner strength.

Emil and Karl by Yankey Glatshteyn.
Translated by Jeffrey Shandler.
Roaring Brook Press
ISBN: 1696431199

This story of two boys left alone in Vienna after their parents have been arrested by the Nazis is particularly significant because it was the first book written for children about the Holocaust. It was published in the United States in Yiddish in 1940 before the full horrors of World War II had unfolded. Shandler's seamless translation now makes the story accessible to contemporary readers.

Hiding Edith: A True Story by Kathy Kacer. (Holocaust Remembrance)
Second Story Press
ISBN: 1897187068

Through the story of Edith Schwalb Gelbard, who survived the Holocaust by continually moving and hiding, the reader can relate to the situation in Europe before World War II, the plight of the Jews, the virtue of righteous gentiles who helped them, and the courage and strength it took to survive.

In the Days of Sand and Stars by Marlee Pinsker.
Illustrations by François Thisdale.
Tundra Books
ISBN: 0887767249

A compilation of stories, in the tradition of *Midrash*, about the everyday lives and personalities of the biblical women Eve, Naamah, Sarah, Rebecca, Leah, Rachel, Dina and Yocheved.

The Cat with the Yellow Star: Coming of Age in Terezin by Susan Goldman Rubin with Ela Weissberger.
Holiday House
ISBN: 0823418316

This impressively researched photographic memoir tells of a young girl from Czechoslovakia who studied with Friedl Dicker-Brandeis and participated in the children's opera *Brundibar* at the Terezin concentration camp during World War II.

A Pickpocket's Tale by Karen Schwabach.
Random House
ISBN: 037583379X

In 1730, Molly is a ten-year-old orphan who is convicted of pick-pocketing in London and deported to America. When a Jewish family purchases her to be their indentured servant, Molly learns to follow and respect the Jewish traditions and also learns about the importance of family, forgiveness, and faith.

Stealing Home by Ellen Schwartz.
Tundra Books
ISBN: 0887767656

Nine-year-old Joey Sexton, living in the Bronx in 1947, is orphaned after the death of his mother. When his aunt welcomes him into her home, the rest of the family and their neighbors aren't as accepting of Joey's bi-racial heritage. Inspired by Jackie Robinson, Joey learns how to shake off the taunts of the neighborhood bullies, grains an appreciation for his Jewish heritage, and builds a loving and respectful relationship with his grandfather.

Teen Readers

Lilith's Ark: Teenage Tales of Biblical Women by Deborah Bodin Cohen.
Jewish Publication Society
ISBN: 0827608330

This collection of stories about Jewish matriarchs and other women associated with the book of Genesis includes Lilith, Eve, Sarah, Hagar, Rebekah, Rachel, Leah, Dinah, Tamar, and Asenath. The discussion guide for each chapter consists of themes, questions, and a mother-daughter dialogue.

Notes from the Midnight Driver by Jordan Sonnenblick.
Scholastic
ISBN: 0439757797

Alex Gregory gets drunk, takes his mother's car, and crashes into a lawn gnome. He must pay his debt to society by doing 100 hours of community service in a nursing home attending to Sol Lewis, a cantankerous resident who suffers from emphysema.

***The Unresolved* by T. K. Welsh.**
Dutton Books
ISBN: 0525477314

The spirit of Mallory Meer, a teenage girl who died on the General Slocum, haunts those involved with the 1904 disaster. While history records that a fire started and spread quickly, this work of fiction explores what might have happened when two love struck teenagers steal a moment together below deck and another vents his jealousy by causing the blaze and blaming his nemesis.

2006 Awards

Younger Readers

***Sholom's Treasure: How Sholom Aleichem Became a Writer* by Erica Silverman.**
Illustrations by Mordicai Gerstein.
Farrar, Straus and Giroux
ISBN: 0374380554

Chronicles Sholom Aleichem's childhood, revealing the influences that turned him into the great Yiddish writer who would give us the story that became *Fiddler on the Roof.* This is a vital, engaging, living-and-breathing portrait of one of modern Jewish culture's most famous and beloved champions.

Older Readers

***Confessions of a Closet Catholic* by Sarah Littman.**
Dutton Children's Books
ISBN: 0525473653

Justine Silver struggles to balance her family's expectations that she should be Jewish "but not too Jewish." Frustrated, she follows a Catholic friend's example by giving up Judaism for Lent, and thus begins a search for identity and belonging that will resonate with readers of all religions.

Honor Books

Younger Readers

The Journey that Saved Curious George: The True Wartime Escape of Margret and H.A. Rey by Louise Borden.
Illustrations by Allan Drummond.
Houghton Mifflin
ISBN: 0618339248

This delightfully written story tells how Margret and H.A. Rey escaped from Nazi-occupied France in 1940, carrying in their bicycle baskets the manuscripts that would become their beloved picture books about Curious George, the little monkey.

Ruth and Naomi: A Bible Story by Jean Marzollo.
Little, Brown
ISBN: 0316741396

In all of her biblical retellings, this author condenses details while preserving the stories' spirit and meaning. This one exemplifies *chesed* (lovingkindness), shown by Ruth and Naomi's caring for one another and by the kindness extended to them by Boaz.

Shlemiel Crooks by Anna Olswanger.
Illustrtaions by Paula Goodman Koz.
Junebug Books
ISBN: 158838165X

Told with Yiddish inflected English, sprinkled with familiar Jewish curses and words, Anna Olswanger elaborates on the true story of the attempted robbery of her great-grandfather's saloon in St. Louis in 1919.

Kibitzers and Fools: Tales My Zayda Told Me by Simms Taback.
Viking,
ISBN: 0670059552

Brimming with humor and bursting with life, this dynamically illustrated collection of anecdotes and short stories about *kibitzers, shlemiels, noodniks, meshuganers* and other Yiddish types is reminiscent of Taback's award winning *Joseph Had a Little Overcoat*.

Older Readers

Memories of Survival by Esther Nisenthal Krinitz and Bernice Steinhardt.
Hyperion Books for Children
ISBN: 0786851260

Esther Nisenthal Krinitz retells the story of her childhood in a small Polish village through a series of hand-stitched embroidered panels.

The King of Mulberry Street by Donna Jo Napoli.
Wendy Lamb Books, an imprint of Random House
ISBN: 0385746539

This powerful historical novel about an Italian-Jewish immigrant child reveals to readers that just 100 years ago, children as young as eight came to this country alone, with nothing but their wits and good luck to help them survive.

Prince William, Maximilian Minsky, and Me by Holly-Jane Rahlens.
Candlewick Press
ISBN: 0763627046

Nelly Sue Edelmeister learns to play basketball, copes with a major crush on Prince William, makes a true friend, and finds meaning in becoming a bat mitzvah in this funny and touching novel that takes place in modern Berlin.

The Travels of Benjamin of Tudela: Through Three Continents in the Twelfth Century by Uri Shulevitz.
Farrar, Straus and Giroux
ISBN: 0374377545

Known only from the book he wrote about his travels, Benjamin left Spain in 1159 and spent fourteen years traveling. This beautifully illustrated chronicle describes and shows a 12th century world as it might have been experienced by Benjamin of Tudela, complete with muddy roads, searing deserts, walled cities and mighty seas.

Teen Readers

No books recognized in this category.

Notable Books

Younger Readers

Love Me Later by Julie Baer.
Bollix Books
ISBN: 1932188037

A tender slice of life story that reveals family love and the wonders of childhood for a boy who just happens to be Jewish.

Hanukkah Shmanukkah! by Esme Raji Codell.
Illustrations by LeUyen Pham.
Hyperion Books for Children
ISBN: 0786851791

An adaptation of Dickens' Christmas Carol with protagonist old Scroogenmacher visited by three ghostly rabbis who take him back in time to the Maccabees, to present day tenements (early 20th century) and then on to the future. Will he get the message?

The Seventh Day: A Shabbat Story by Deborah Bodin Cohen.
Illustrations by Melanie W. Hall.
Kar-Ben Publishing
ISBN: 158013125

The story of creation is told with God as potter, painter and musician. After much hard work, there is a joyous "whole world" celebration of Shabbat. Beautiful mixed media illustrations enhance this metaphorical version of the creation myth.

A Box of Candles by Laurie Jacobs.
Illustrations by Shelly Ephraim.
Boyds Mills Press
ISBN: 1590781694

Seven-year-old Ruthie learns about the annual Jewish cycle of Sabbaths and holidays when her grandmother gives her a candlestick and a box of candles. She also learns about accepting others as Grandma Gussie and Mr. Adler begin spending a lot of time together.

It's Purim Time! by Latifa Berry Kropf.
Photographs by Tod Cohen.
Kar-Ben Publishing
ISBN: 1580131530

Another in the holiday series, this photo essay depicts the history and customs of the holiday including crafts (*graggers* and costumes), snacks and a reading of the story of Queen Esther.

In God's Hands **by Lawrence Kushner and Gary Schmidt.**
Illustrations by Matthew J. Baek.
Jewish Lights Publishing
ISBN: 1580232248

A delightful retelling of the legend of the loaves in the synagogue Torah ark, beautifully illustrated.

Dreamer from the Village: The Story of Marc Chagall **by Michelle Markel.**
Illustrations by Emily Lisker.
Henry Holt
ISBN: 0805063730

Introduces young readers to the life of Marc Chagall beginning with his birth in a small Russian village, his childhood, his family's observances of the Jewish holidays, and the development of his artistic talent, despite being discouraged and unappreciated by his family. Lisker's Chagall inspired illustrations beautifully depict the places and characters of Chagall's life.

Jerusalem Sky: Stars, Crosses, and Crescents **by Mark Podwal.**
Doubleday Books for Young Readers
ISBN: 038574689X

A poetic evocation of the sky over the world's most beloved city shows that the love borne by Jews, Christians, and Muslims for Jerusalem can be something that brings us together instead of tearing us apart.

The Ark **by Matthew Reinhart.**
Simon & Schuster Children's Publishing
ISBN: 0689859090

Stunning and intricate three-dimensional pop-ups bring the story of Noah's Ark to life.

Before You Were Born by Howard Schwartz.
Illustrations by Kristina Swarner.
Roaring Brook Press
ISBN: 1596430281

With sophisticated, lyrical prose, noted storyteller Howard Schwartz retells the *Midrash* of the angel Lailah.

The Matzoh Ball Boy by Lisa Shulman.
Illustrations by Rosanne Litzinger.
Penguin Group
ISBN: 0525471693

A new take of "The Gingerbread Boy" as Bubbe's matzoh ball is off to see the world with an interesting twist at the end. Glossary included.

It's Tu B'Shevat by Edie Stoltz Zolkower.
Kar-Ben Publishing
ISBN: 1580131271

The simply, rhyming text of this board book beings with "Grab a shovel. Pick a spot. Plant a tree, it's Tu B'Shevat!" and continues as a young boy and his family plant a tree, say a blessing, enjoy the shade, the fruit, and the birds, and watch the tree grow.

Older Readers

The JGirls' Guide: The Young Jewish Woman's Handbook for Coming of Age by **Penina Adelman, Ali Feldman and Shulamit Reinharz.**
Jewish Lights Publishing
ISBN: 1580232159

For the teen or preteen girl who asks "Where do I fit in?," this includes lessons based on mitzvoth, interpretations of text, diary entries, and the views of young girls on contemporary issues.

The Hebrew Kid and the Apache Maiden by **Robert J. Avrech.**
Seraphic Press
ISBN: 0975438212

In the years following the Civil War, twelve-year-old Ariel Isaacson and his family, Jewish immigrants from Russia are kicked out of their Arizona town by an anti-Semitic mayor and townspeople, and are forced to embark on a difficult and dangerous journey through the unsettled Arizona territory.

Hitler Youth: Growing Up in Hitler's Shadow by **Susan Campbell Bartoletti.**
Scholastic
ISBN: 0439353793

This well-researched, large format book describes the rise of Hitler and the Nazi Party, and World War II and its aftermath, through the eyes of twelve ordinary young people in Germany including those who participated in the Hitler Youth movement and those who resisted.

Four Sides, Eight Nights: A New Spin on Hanukkah by **Rebecca Tova Ben-Zvi.**
Illustrations by Susanna Natti.
Roaring Brook Press
ISBN: 1596430591

A delightful exploration of the science, traditions, customs, and meaning of Hanukkah, with the dreidel used as a sort of road map.

Genius: A Photobiography of Albert Einstein by **Marfe Ferguson Delano.**
National Geographic Children's Books
ISBN: 0792295447

Meet the 20th century's most important scientist in this very attractive book and learn that the man with the big brain also had a big heart. Delano achieves a stunning balance between words and sepia-toned photos.

Bridge to America by **Linda Glaser.**
Houghton Mifflin Company
ISBN: 0618563016

Young Fivel and his family endure hunger, cold, fear and poverty in a Polish shtetl while waiting to hear from his father in America. Once in America, Fivel must adjust to Minnesota and learn to appreciate his past.

A Promise Fulfilled: Theodor Herzl, Chaim Weitzmann, and David Ben-Gurion, and the Creation of the State of Israel by **Howard Greenfeld.**
Greenwillow Books
ISBN: 006051504X

An engrossing account of three very different men who were central to the founding of modern Israel.

Broken Soup by Kathryn Lasky.
Viking
ISBN: 0670059315

A historical novel set in the Russian Pale of Settlement in the late 1800s shows the conditions that led to massive Jewish emigration from Russia. A companion to Lasky's 1981 award-winning book *The Night Journey*.

Hidden Child by Isaac Millman.
Farrar, Straus and Giroux
ISBN: 0374330719

This unique, large format personal narrative beautifully tells the story of the author's experience as a hidden child in Nazi-occupied France during World War II. Well-captioned black and white photographs along with double-spread full-color composite paintings accompany the first-person narration.

Zayda Was a Cowboy by June Levitt Nislick.
Jewish Publication Society
ISBN: 0817608179

When their grandfather moves in with them, Bill and Danny are off put by his habits, but are then fascinated by his stories of immigration from Russia and work as a cowboy in Texas.

Anne Frank by Josephine Poole.
Illustrations by Angela Barrett.
Alfred A. Knopf, an imprint of Random House
ISBN: 0375832424

Depicts the life of Anne Frank as a young girl in Frankfurt, Germany and in Amsterdam--her experiences in school, her friend, and her life in hiding. The illustrations are beautiful and haunting, with intricate detail they show how Anne changes, grows and matures into a young woman.

The Secret Seder by Doreen Rappaport.
Illustrations by Emily Arnold McCully.
Hyperion Books for Children
ISBN: 0786807776

Jacques, a young French boy whose family lives as Catholics during World War II, attends a secret Seder with his father in a secluded cabin, where despite the danger and meager menu, the participants are inspired and hopeful.

***The Flag with Fifty-Six Stars* by Susan Goldman Rubin.**
Illustrations by Bill Farnsworth.
Holiday House
ISBN: 0823416534

Through extensive research, eyewitness accounts and personal interviews, Goldman tells the inspiring, moving, and hopeful story of a group of prisoners in the Mauthausen concentration camp who secretly created an American flag to present to the liberating forces.

***Always Remember Me: How One Family Survived World War II* by Marisabina Russo.**
Atheneum Books for Young Readers
ISBN: 0689869207

Russo relates the experiences of her own family, and how love helped them survive the Holocaust.

***Lost in America* by Marilyn Sachs.**
Roaring Brook Press
ISBN: 1596430400

Thirty-two years after the publication of *A Pocket Full of Seeds* (1973), Marilyn Sachs continues the story of Nicole Nieman focusing on the end of World War II and Nicole's experiences as a new immigrant in America.

***Light Years* by Tammar Stein.**
Alfred A. Knopf, an imprint of Random House
ISBN: 0375830235

Twenty-year-old Maya Laor is on her way to meet her boyfriend Dov to tell him that she has decided to leave Israel to study at the University of Virginia when he is killed by a suicide bomber. In alternating chapters between Virginia and Israel, Tammar Stein pieces together Maya and Dov's relationship, Maya's life in Israel, her army service, and her family.

***Double Crossing: A Jewish Immigration Story* by Eve Tal.**
Cinco Puntos Press
ISBN: 0938317946

Raizel and her father face rejection at Ellis Island, but with a change in attitude and the help of kindly fellow passengers, their second attempt at immigration is successful. Based on a true story.

When I Was a Soldier: A Memoir by Valerie Zenatti.
Translated by Adriana Hunter.
Bloomsbury USA
ISBN: 1582349789

The memoir of an Israeli girl thrust from her typical teenage life into compulsory military service, where she learns to adapt to the physical rigors and emotional challenges.

Teen Readers

No books recognized in this category.

2005 - Dating system changed this year to reflect year in which award is announced instead of year of publication. Award-giving did NOT skip a year.

2004 Awards

Younger Readers

N.B.: In the Younger Reader category, there was no award winner.

Older Readers

Real Time by Pnina Moed Kass.
Clarion Books
ISBN: 0618442030

In this powerful and compelling young adult novel, the lives of sixteen different characters, spanning several countries and continents, intersect over the course of six days preceding and following a bus bombing in present day Jerusalem.

Honor Books

Younger Readers

Daniel in the Lions' Den by Jean Marzollo.
Little, Brown
ISBN: 0316741329

A simple retelling of the Biblical tale about faith, courage, and heroism introduces the Bible story while a column of ants at the bottom of each page comments on events.

Older Readers

Daniel, Half-Human by David Chotjewitz.
Translated by Doris Orgel.
Atheneum Books for Young Readers
ISBN: 0689857470

In 1933, best friends Daniel and Armin admire Hitler, but as anti-Semitism buoys Hitler to power, Daniel learns he is half Jewish, threatening the friendship even as life in their beloved Hamburg, Germany, is becoming nightmarish.

Bobbie Rosenfeld: The Olympian Who Could Do Everything by **Anne Dublin.**
Second Story Press
ISBN: 1896764827

With clear, concise writing, an easy, conversational tone, relevant and helpful text boxes, and interesting photographs and illustrations, Anne Dublin not only tells the story of Bobbie Rosenfeld but provides an impressive history of Canadian women's sports. She also puts Bobbie's life in perspective by providing background information about Canadian and world history and culture, and supplies details about Bobbie's Jewish background and identity.

The Cats in Krasinski Square by **Karen Hesse.**
Illustrations by Wendy Watson.
Scholastic
ISBN: 0439435404

Two Jewish sisters, escapees of the infamous Warsaw Ghetto, devise a plan to thwart an attempt by the Gestapo to intercept food bound for starving people behind the dark Wall.

Wonders and Miracles: A Passover Companion by **Eric Kimmel.**
Scholastic
ISBN: 0439071755

Presents the steps performed in a traditional Passover Seder, plus stories, songs, poetry, and art that spans 3,000 years, four continents, and fifteen countries – a book for the whole family to read before and during the holiday.

My Guardian Angel by **Sylvie Weil.**
Translated by Gillian Rosner.
Scholastic
ISBN: 0439576814

In 11th century Troyes, France, Elvina, the unusual granddaughter of renowned Jewish rabbi Solomon ben Isaac (Rashi), who prefers studying and writing to activities considered respectable for girls, takes a great risk by helping a young boy who has run away from a group of Christian Crusaders.

Notable Books

Younger Readers

The Mystery Bear: A Purim Story by Leone Adelson.
Illustrations by Naomi Howland.
Clarion Books
ISBN: 0618337253

A young bear is mistaken for a costumed reveler when he wakes up from his winter sleep and follows the wonderful smells coming from a cottage where the townspeople are celebrating Purim.

Papa's Latkes by Michelle Edwards.
Illustrations by Stacey Schuett.
Candlewick
ISBN: 0763607797

A sad, sweet and unsentimental story that takes place at Hanukkah, the first a father and his two daughters have observed since Mama died.

Mrs. Greenberg's Messy Hanukkah by Linda Glaser.
Illustrations by Nancy Cote.
Albert Whitman
ISBN: 1930143877

Instead of going with her parents to do errands on the first night of Hanukkah, Rachel visits Mrs. Greenberg next door and proceeds to mess up her immaculate kitchen while making potato latkes.

What You Will See Inside a Synagogue by Lawrence A. Hoffman and Ron Wolfson.
Illustrations by Bill Aron.
Jewish Lights Publishing
ISBN: 2895074127

A short introduction to the Jewish religion precedes many photographs that how what goes on in Reform, Conservative and Reconstructionist synagogues in North America, such as prayer, life cycle events, and holidays.

The Coat of Many Colors by Jenny Koralek.
Illustrations by Pauline Baynes.
Eerdmans
ISBN: 0802852777

A simple retelling of the biblical story of Joseph, boldly illustrated.

It's Sukkah Time! by Latifa Berry Kropf.
Photographs by Tod Cohen.
Kar-Ben Publishing
ISBN: 1580130844

Photographs of preschoolers decorating a sukkah and celebrating the holiday make this book a delight. Don't miss Kropf's other 2004 holiday books, *It's Seder Time!* and *It's Hanukkah Time!*

David and Goliath by Jean Marzollo.
Little Brown
ISBN: 0316471388

A simple retelling of the biblical story of David and Goliath, with talking lambs at the bottom of each page.

Jonah and the Whale (and the Worm) by Jean Marzollo.
Little Brown
ISBN: 0316471345

The biblical story of Jonah is told with the help of a worm and the octopus at the bottom of each page.

Miriam and Her Brother Moses by Jean Marzollo.
Little Brown
ISBN: 0316741310

The biblical story of Moses' adoption has fish giving commentary at the bottom of each page.

Apples and Pomegranates: A Family Seder for Rosh Hashanah by Rahel Musleah.
Illustrations by Judy Jarrett.
Kar-Ben Publishing
ISBN: 1580131239

Musleah gives us a complete Seder for the Rosh Hashanah holiday, including background information, stories, and songs, all centered upon special foods from different Jewish communities around the world.

Where Do People Go When They Die? by Mindy Avra Portnoy.
Illustrations by Shelly O. Haas.
Kar-Ben Publishing
ISBN: 158013081X

A variety of answers to the title question, "where do people go when they die?" are offered appropriately for young children.

Older Readers

The Kids' Catalog of Hanukkah by David A. Adler.
Jewish Publication Society
ISBN: 0827608055

Another title in the *Kids' Catalog* series, focusing on Hanukkah and filled with facts, stories, songs, games, recipes, and crafts.

The Mystery of the Dead Sea Scrolls by Hagit Allon and Lena Zehavi.
Illustrations by Yossi Abulafia.
Jewish Publication Society
ISBN: 0152163913

In this over-sized illustrated chapter book, readers follow the adventures of Daniel, an eleven-year-old boy living in contemporary Jerusalem, as he works on a project for school about the Dead Sea Scrolls.

Walking the Bible: an Illustrated Journey for Kids by Bruce Feiler.
Illustrations by Sasha Meret.
HarperCollins
ISBN: 0060511176

Feiler, accompanied by Israeli archaeologist Avner Goren, visits places in the Middle East where biblical stories may have taken place including the Creation story, Garden of Eden, Noah's Ark, Exodus, and the receiving of the Ten Commandments.

Israel in Pictures by Margaret J. Goldstein.
Lerner
ISBN: 1580130887

This revised overview of Israel, which is part of the Visual Geography series, focuses on the geography and history of both ancient and modern Israel. It includes a timeline, suggested websites, and an index.

Duel by David Grossman.
Translated by Betsy Rosenberg.
Bloomsbury
ISBN: 1582349304

David attempts to unravel the mystery between two elderly men who he meets in the Hebrew Home for the Aged while doing community service.

The Harmonica by Tony Johnston.
Illustrations by Ron Mazellan.
Charlesbridge
ISBN: 1570915474
A young boy survives in a concentration camp because he can play Shubert on his harmonica, which the commandant asks for every night.

The Underground Reporters by Kathy Kacer.
Second Story Press
ISBN: 1896764851

A group of Jewish children in a small town in Czechoslovakia publish a newspaper called Klepy or "gossip" in Czech, during World War II, until they are deported to concentration camps.

The Dog of Knots by Kathy Walden Kaplan.
Eerdmans
ISBN: 0802852599

A slice of life in Haifa, Israel during the time of the Yom Kippur War as told through the eyes of Mayim, a young Jewish girl.

Quake! Disaster in San Francisco, 1906 by Gail Langer Karwoski.
Illustrations by Robert Papp.
Peachtree Publishers
ISBN: 1561453102

The 1906 San Francisco earthquake is the backdrop for a story of two thirteen-year-old boys -- one Jewish, one Chinese -- who have banded together along with a stray dog, in search of their respective families from whom they were separated.

Rosie in Los Angeles: Action! By Carol Matas.
Aladdin, an imprint of Simon & Schuster
ISBN: 0689857160

Rosie finds adventure when her family moves to the foothills of Los Angeles to start their own film production company. This third book in the series follows *Rosie in New York: Gotcha!* And *Rosie in Chicago: Play Ball!*

Esther by Sharon E. McKay.
Penguin Canada
ISBN: 0143312049

Esther, a young Jewish girl in 18th century France, must conceal her real identity to survive and disguises herself as a boy in order to become the first Jew to arrive in New France.

Albert Einstein by Stephanie McPherson.
Lerner
ISBN: 1580130941

An upbeat biography of Einstein using anecdotes and photographs.

The Queen of Persia by Moshe Moscowitz.
Illustrations by David Sokoloff.
Shazak Productions
ISBN: 1930925093

A lively "graphic novel" presentation of the story of Purim

Missing Persons: The Chocolate Lover by M.E. Rabb.
Speak, an imprint of Penguin Putnam
ISBN: 0142500429

Teenaged Jewish sisters Sam and Sophie Shattenberg change their identities as they flee from New York to a small town in Indiana and open a detective agency. *The Chocolate Lover* is full of Jewish flavor, but the focus is on the solving of mysteries. Don't miss the rest of the *Missing Persons* series: *The Rose Queen*, *The Venetian Policeman* and *The Unsuspecting Gourmet.*

Six Million Paper Clips by Peter W. Schroeder and Dagmar Schroeder-Hildebrand.
Kar-Ben Publishing
ISBN: 1580131697

One teacher's desire to teach about intolerance led to a three-year project in which the entire community of Whitwell, Tennessee participated, culminating in the building of a Holocaust memorial.

Your Travel Guide to Ancient Israel by Josepha Sherman.
Lerner
ISBN: 0822530724

Written as a time travel log back to an ancient culture, the reader can experience daily life in Ancient Israel.

Ilan Ramon: Israel's Space Hero by **Barbara Sofer.**
Kar-Ben Publishing
ISBN: 1580131158

This basic biography covers Ilan Ramon's childhood, his Bar Mitzvah, his service in the Israeli Air Force, and his path to becoming the first Israeli astronaut, with details about his family, friends and colleagues.

Ilan Ramon: Jewish Star by **Devra Newberger Speregen.**
Jewish Publication Society
ISBN: 0827607695

A well-written biography of Ilan Ramon concentrating on his military career and life as an astronaut.

Matzah Meals: A Passover Cookbook for Kids (**revised edition**) **by Judy Steinberg and Barbara Tabs.**
Illustrations by Bill Hauser.
Kar-Ben Publishing
ISBN: 1580130860

Good advice to young cooks plus suggestions and crafts for the Seder are the prelude to this collection of recipes that range from the no-cooking variety for young children to more complicated ones for teens.

2003 Awards

Younger Readers

Bagels from Benny **by Aubrey Davis.**
Illustrations by Dušan Petričić.
Kids Can Press
ISBN: 1553374177
After accepting the compliments for the tasty bagels made at the family bakery, Benny's grandfather explains that God is really to thank for the delicious creations, causing Benny to begin leaving a bag of bagels for God every week at the synagogue as a demonstration of his gratitude.

Older Readers

Who Was The Woman Who Wore The Hat? **by Nancy Patz.**
Dutton
ISBN: 0525469990

Offers a reflection on a woman's hat that was on display in the Jewish Historical Museum in Amsterdam that questions who the woman might have been, what her life may have been like, and how she may have ended up a Holocaust victim.

Honor Books
Younger Readers

The Moses Basket **by Jenny Koralek.**
Illustrations by Pauline Baynes.
Eerdmans
ISBN: 0802852513

A simple retelling of how Moses, who grew to lead the Hebrews out of captivity in Egypt, was saved when his mother and sister set him adrift in a water-tight basket where Pharoah's daughter would find him.

Chanukah on the Prairie **by Burt E. Schuman.**
Illustrations by Rosalind Charney Kaye.
UAHC
ISBN: 080740814X

After the Zalcman family immigrates to Grand Forks, North Dakota, they are welcomed by the local Jewish community and celebrate their first Chanukah on the prairie.

When the Chickens Went on Strike: A Rosh Hashanah Tale by Erica Silverman.
Illustrations by Matthew Trueman.
Dutton
ISBN: 0525468625

A Jewish boy living in Russia learns a lesson from the village chickens at the time of Rosh Hashanah, the Jewish New Year.

Older Readers

Ancient Israelites and Their Neighbors: An Activity Guide by Marian Broida.
Chicago Review Press
ISBN: 1556524579

Examines the ancient cultures of the Israelites, the Philistines, and the Phoenicians, focusing on art, architecture, food, clothing, writing, history, religion, and work. Includes related activities.

Tough Questions Jews Ask: a Young Adult's Guide to Building a Jewish Life by Edward Feinstein.
Jewish Lights Publishing
ISBN: 158023139X

Provides questions and answers for some major concerns facing Jewish youths, and includes explanations about such issues as God, prayer, good and evil, and the afterlife.

Birdland by Tracy Mack.
Scholastic
ISBN: 0439535905

Fourteen-year-old, tongue-tied Jed spends winter break working on a school project filming a documentary about his East Village, New York City, neighborhood, where he is continually reminded of his older brother, Zeke, a promising poet who died the year before.

Notable Books

Younger Readers

I Only Like What I Like by Julie Baer.
Bollix Books
ISBN: 1932188002

Vignettes about childhood likes and dislikes are strikingly illustrated with quilt-like designs whose images, lines, and colors evoke a small child's imaginative perception of his world.

Long Johns for a Small Chicken by Esther Silverstein Blanc and Godeane Eagle.
Illustrations by Tennessee Dixon.
Volcano Press
ISBN 1884244238

When a fierce Nebraska hailstorm batters a little chick, Mama makes him his own pair of long johns to keep him warm. The vintage setting, kindness, and humor of the story are captured in its illustrations.

Avram's Gift by Margie Blumberg.
Illustrations by Laurie McGaw.
MB Publishing
ISBN: 0962416622

A well-illustrated chapter book that affirms the values of family, tradition, and continuity. The sounding of the shofar during the High Holidays is an important part of the plot.

A Sweet Year: a Taste of the Jewish Holidays by Mark Podwal.
Doubleday
ISBN: 0385746377

A lyrically written and rather sophisticated look at the Jewish holidays through the food traditionally associated with each of them. Podwal's gouache and acrylic paintings are inspired.

Five Alive! My Yom Tov Five Senses by Dina Rosenfeld.
Illustrations by Tova Leff.
Hachai Publishing
ISBN: 1029628064

Through a simply rhyming story and cheerful illustrations, young children are encouraged to see, hear, smell, taste and touch some of the major Jewish holidays.

Tali's Jerusalem Scrapbook by Sylvia Rouss.
Illustrations by Nancy Oppenheimer.
Pitspopany Press
ISBN: 1930143699

An Israeli child's feelings about the conflict in her beloved city are explored in this illustrated story.

Turn, Turn, Turn by Pete Seeger.
Illustrations by Wendy Anderson Halperin.
Simon & Schuster
ISBN: 0689852355

Readers will turn, turn, turn their heads to appreciate all of the details in the circular illustrations that complement passages from Ecclesiastes made into a song by Pete Seeger. An audio CD is included.

The Passover. Seder by Emily Sper.
Cartwheel, an imprint of Scholastic
ISBN: 0439443121

Lift the flaps, rub the textures, turn the wheels, and pull the tabs to learn about the Seder and a few Hebrew words.

It's a Miracle! A Hanukkah Storybook by Stephanie Spinner.
Illustrations by Jill McElmurry.
Atheneum
ISBN: 068984493X

Those bedtime stories that Grandma Karen tells Owen during Hanukkah remind him of people he knows. At a family celebration on the eighth night, he finds out for sure that the story characters are his very own relatives!

Something for Nothing by Ann Redisch Stampler.
Illustrations by Jacqueline M. Cohen.
Clarion Books
ISBN: 0618159827

In a captivating trickster tale, a peace-loving dog foils three rowdy cats who terrorize the neighborhood by playing upon their greed. This wry look at the oft-disturbed peace of the Eastern European *shtetl* is beautifully illustrated.

***Rachel's Gift* by Richard Ungar.**
Tundra Books
ISBN: 0887766161

The prophet Elijah appears in many guises and only young Rachel realizes that he has visited her house and left a very precious gift.

Older Readers

***Golda Meir* by Anna Claybourne.**
Heinemann Library
ISBN: 1403408351

The life of Golda Meir and the history of modern Israel are inseparably woven into this readable biography.

***My Grandmother's Stories: A Collection of Jewish Folktales* by Adèle Geras. Illustrations by Anita Lobel.**
Alfred A. Knopf, an imprint of Random House
ISBN: 0375922857

Sparkling new illustrations grace this collection of Jewish folktales. An earlier edition illustrated by another artist won the Sydney Taylor Book Award in 1990.

***The Stone Lamp: Eight Stories of Hanukkah through History* by Karen Hesse. Illustrations by Brian Pinkney.**
Hyperion Books
ISBN: 0786806192

Narrative poems about times of crisis in Jewish history. Striking illustrations and very discussable!

***Shutting Out the Sky: Life in the Tenements of New York: 1880-1924* by Deborah Hopkinson.**
Orchard Books, an imprint of Scholastic
ISBN: 0439375908

Documentary photographs and the voices of five young immigrants transport readers into the teeming streets and crowded tenements of New York's Lower East Side.

Brundibar by Tony Kushner.
Illustrations by Maurice Sendak.
Michael Di Capua Books, an imprint of Hyperion
ISBN: 0786809043

A sassy narrative style and splendid, multi-meaningful illustrations capture both the fairy tale charm and the underlying menace of a children's opera that was performed by prisoners in the Terezin concentration camp.

Room in the Heart by Sonia Levitin.
Dutton
ISBN: 0525468714

The German occupation of Denmark and its impact on a circle of middle class families -- Jewish and non-Jewish -- compel them to act on their beliefs.

Rosie in New York City: Gotcha! by Carol Matas
Aladdin, and imprint of Simon & Schuster
ISBN: 0689857144

It's 1909 and plucky Rosie becomes a labor organizer, participating in the making of the American Jewish community. The first in a series.

The Enemy Has a Face by Gloria Miklowitz.
Eerdmans
ISBN: 0802852432

An Israeli teenager's disappearance propels this suspenseful story that reveals some of the tensions in Israeli-Palestinian relations. The Los Angeles setting brings the conflict home to American teens; the ending is painful.

Abraham Joshua Heschel: Man of Spirit, Man of Action by Or Rose.
Jewish Publication Society
ISBN: 082760758X

The life and work of one of the 20th century's most important Jewish thinkers are introduced.

Murder at the 1972 Olympics in Munich by Liz Sonneborn.
Rosen Publishing
ISBN: 0823936546

A detailed account of the Palestinian terrorist attack on a group of Israeli athletes and its aftermath.

Milkweed by Jerry Spinelli.
Alfred A. Knopf, an imprint of Random House
ISBN: 0375813748

The horrors of the Warsaw Ghetto are plumbed in this powerful story about a homeless, orphan boy who survives by stealing food and whose first real experience of love is for a doomed Jewish family.

Ilan Ramon: Israel's First Astronaut by Tanya Stone.
Millbrook Press
ISBN: 0761328882

Israeli hero, role model and mensch -- Ilan Ramon fits all descriptions, as this poignant biography makes clear.

Luba: The Angel of Bergen-Belsen by Luba Tryszynska-Frederick. As told to Michelle McCann.
Illustrations by Ann Marshall.
Tricycle Press
ISBN: 1582460981

Deeply colored, dramatic illustrations enhance this true story of a woman who rescued and risked her life to save a group of abandoned Jewish children in a Nazi concentration camp.

Marc Chagall by Jude Welton.
Franklin Watts
ISBN: 0531166457
The artist's long, productive and exciting life is documented with family photographs and handsome illustrations.

2002 Awards

Younger Readers

Chicken Soup. by Heart by Esther Hershenhorn.
Illustrations by Rosanne Litzinger.
Simon and Schuster Books for Young Readers
ISBN: 0689826656

When Rudie's sitter gets the flu, he uses her recipe to make her a batch of special chicken soup, including the secret recipe of stories from the heart.

Older Readers

Hana's Suitcase: A True Story by Karen Levine.
Second Story Press, 2002. ISBN: 189676455X
Albert Whitman & Company, 2003. ISBN: 0807531480

A biography of a Czech girl who died in the Holocaust, told in alternating chapters with an account of how the curator of a Japanese Holocaust center learned about her life after Hana's suitcase was sent to her.

Honor Books

Younger Readers

Noah's Ark by Jerry Pinkney.
SeaStar, an imprint of North-South Books
ISBN: 587172011

Retells the biblical story of the great flood and how Noah and his family faithfully responded to God's call to save animal life on earth.

Sammy Spider's First Trip to Israel: A Book about the Five Senses by Sylvia Rouss.
Illustrations by Katherine Janus Kahn.
Kar-Ben Publishing
ISBN: 1580130356

Sammy Spider joins the Shapiro family on a vacation, and he uses his five senses to experience Israel.

Pearl's Passover: A Family Celebration through Stories, Recipes, Crafts, and Songs by **Jane Breskin Zalben.**
Simon and Schuster Books for Young Readers
ISBN: 0689814879

As an extended family prepares for their Passover celebration, they explain the various customs and traditions related to this holiday.

Older Readers

One Candle by **Eve Bunting.**
Illustrations by K. Wendy Popp.
Joanna Cotler Books, an imprint of HarperCollins
ISBN: 0060281154

Every year a family celebrates Hanukkah by retelling the story of how Grandma and her sister managed to mark the day while in a German concentration camp.

A Picture of Grandmother by **Esther Hautzig.**
Illustrations by Beth Peck.
Frances Foster, an imprint of Farrar, Straus and Giroux
ISBN: 0374359202

A letter inviting Sara's mother and grandmother to come from Poland to America and mentioning a mysterious photograph arouses Sara's curiosity and leads her to discover a family secret.

Smoke and Ashes: the Story of the Holocaust Revised and Expanded by **Barbara Rogasky.**
Holiday House
ISBN: 0823416771

An account of the tragic fate of the six million Jews killed during the Holocaust is set against a chronicle of the roots of Nazi anti-Semitism Hitler's rise to power, World War II, and the Nazi program of extermination.

Notable Books

Younger Readers

Night Lights: A Sukkot Story by Barbara Diamond Goldin.
Illustrations by Laura Sucher.
UAHC
ISBN: 0807408034

A little boy is scared to sleep outdoors in a sukkah but with his older sister for companionship, he comes to see the stars in the sky as night lights. The new illustrations for a story first published in 1995 are gentle and comforting.

The Beautiful World That God Made by Rhonda Gowler Greene.
Illustrations by Anne Wilson.
Eerdmans Books for Young Readers
ISBN: 0802852130

A free rendering of the Creation story is given by a short, rhyming verse that builds in cumulative detail. Adding drama to the narrative are outstanding ink and collage illustrations.

Matzah Man by Naomi Howland.
Clarion Books, an imprint of Houghton Mifflin
ISBN: 061811750

"Hot from the oven I jumped and ran, so clever and quick, I'm the Matzah Man!" Sprightly illustrations show all of the action in this Passover version of "The Gingerbread Boy."

It's Challah Time! by Latifa Berry Kropf.
Photographs by Tod Cohen.
Kar-Ben Publishing
ISBN: 1500130364

Colorful photographs of adorable children in a real Jewish preschool are engaging companions to a simple text that captures the fun of making challah in preparation for Shabbat.

The Animals and the Ark by Karla Kuskin.
Illustrations by Michael Grejniec.
Atheneum
ISBN: 0689830955

A poem based on the Bible story of Noah's Ark, originally published in 1957, is enhanced with splashy, rollicking illustrations, a creative book design, and a typeface called "Kentucky Fried."

Runaway Dreidel by Lesléa Newman.
Illustrations by Krysten Brooker.
Henry Holt
ISBN: 0805062378

"Twas the first night of Chanukah and on the fifth floor, there was holiday hustling and bustling galore" begins this engaging tale of a dreidel that leads a little boy, his family, and neighbors on a merry chase.

The Sukkah That I Built by Rochel Groner Vorst.
Illustrations by Elizabeth Victor-Elsby.
Hachai   Publishing
ISBN: 1929628072

A read-aloud story modeled on the classic nursery rhyme, "The House That Jack Built." As a little boy smugly relates how he is doing all the building of the sukkah, his bemused family looks on.

Noah's Ark by Anne Wilson.
Chronicle Books
ISBN: 0811835634

Written in a sparse style and illustrated with flat, bright colors and simple lines, this faithful retelling of the biblical account of the flood celebrates obedience to God and the beauty of the world God made.

Older Readers

The Kids' Cartoon Bible by Chaya Burstein.
Jewish Publication Society
ISBN: 0827607296

In a rousing rendition of the Torah, the Prophets and the Writings, the dialogue is colloquial and the cartoon illustrations are often inspired.

Alexandra's Scroll: The Story of the First Hanukkah Illustrations by Stephen
Fieser.
Henry Holt
ISBN: 0805063846

A young female scribe records the political, social, and religious complexities of the
Maccabean world in this believable portrait of a Judean family at war.

*Angels Sweep the Desert Floor: Bible Legends about Moses in the
Wilderness* by Miriam Chaikin.
Illustrations by Alexander Koshkin.
Clarion Books, an imprint ofHoughton Mifflin
ISBN: 0395978254

A companion to the author's *Clouds of Glory* (2001), these stories draw on biblical
text and Midrash to tell how Moses and the liberated Israelites were guided by
angels.

Marika by Andrea Cheng.
Front Street
ISBN: 1886910782

A fifteen-year-old Hungarian girl, nominally Roman Catholic but with Jewish
ancestry, seeks an identity and a way out after the Germans march into Budapest.

Jewish Holidays All Year Round: A Family Treasury by Ilene Cooper.
Illustrations by Elivia Savadier .
Harry N. Abrams, in Association with the Jewish Museum of New York
ISBN: 0810905507

The history and message of each Jewish holiday are combined with stories, legends,
photographs of objects from the Jewish Museum and delightful original
illustrations.

Forged in Freedom: Shaping the Jewish-American Experience by Norman
H. Finkelstein.
Jewish Publication Society
ISBN: 08276074827

From the Dutch colony of New Amsterdam to the nomination of a Jew for Vice
President, Finkelstein surveys trends and highlights events and personalities that
shaped Jewish American history, especially in the 20th century.

And God Cried, Too: A Kid's Book About Healing and Hope by Rabbi Marc Gellman.
Illustration by Harry Bliss.
Harper Trophy, an imprint of HarperCollins
ISBN: 0060098864

Through a fictional dialogue between Mikey, an angel-in-training, and the chief angel, Gabe, the author gives readers honest yet hopeful answers to questions about injustice and evil. Inspired by the attacks of 9/11.

The Life and Death of Adolf Hitler by James C. Giblin.
Clarion Books, an imprint of Houghton Mifflin, 2002
ISBN: 0395903718

This outstanding biography of the 20th century's greatest monster includes information about his legacy of hatred, carried on by neo-Nazis and skinheads.

Auschwitz: The Story of a Nazi Death Camp by Clive A. Lawton.
Candlewick Press
ISBN: 07636115951

The author traces the history of Auschwitz from construction to liberation and comments on its post-war legacy in this visually powerful presentation.

Anne Frank's Story: Her Life Retold for Children by Carol Ann Lee.
Troll Communications
ISBN: 0816774277

The important events in Anne Frank's brief life and the essence of her personality are conveyed to readers of this accessible biography.

Sparks Fly Upward by Carol Matas.
Clarion Books, an imprint of Houghton Mifflin
ISBN: 061859649

A Jewish immigrant girl in Winnipeg, Canada is sent to a foster home after the family farm burns down. Learning to stand up for herself and to make her own decisions doesn't come easy but Rebecca is a plucky heroine.

Too Young for Yiddish by Richard Michelson.
Illustrations by Neil Waldman.
Talewinds, an imprint of Charlesbridge
ISBN: 0881061182

Inspired by the work of Aaron Lansky, founder of the National Yiddish Book Center, this is the story of a boy who learns to love Yiddish from his grandfather , who has almost given up on it.

Jeremiah's Promise: an Adventure in Modern Israel by Kenneth Roseman.
UAHC
ISBN: 0807407879

Readers are presented with choices...and consequences. Signing on here means learning a great deal about Israel, kibbutz life, archaeology, the religious divide, the role of women, diplomacy, and military exploits.

Invisible Kingdoms: Jewish Tales of Angels, Spirits, and Demons by Howard Schwartz.
Illustrations by Stephen Fieser.
HarperCollins
ISBN: 0060278552

Folktales like these have been part of the Jewish oral tradition since biblical times. These tales are simply told but they treat profound human issues from an unaccustomed perspective.

Facing the Music by Eva Vogiel.
Judaica Press
ISBN: 1880582945

In Vogiel's third novel set in an Orthodox girls' school in England in the late 1940's, a caring faculty helps a student adjust to the discovery that she has a twin sister.

The Promised Land: The Birth of the Jewish People by Neil Waldman.
Boyds Mills Press
ISBN: 1563973324

Why have Jews survived? The author presents his views, based on God's promise of Israel to the Jewish people. Evocative illustrations and an unusual book design add interest.

Finding Sophie: A Search for Belonging in Postwar Britain by Irene N. Watts.
Tundra Books
ISBN: 0887766137

Following *Good-bye Marianne* (1999) and *Remember Me* (2000), this riveting novel, set in London, completes the author's "Kindertransport Trilogy."

2001 Awards

Younger Readers

Rivka's First Thanksgiving by Elsa Okon Rael.
Illustrations by Maryann Kovalski.
Margaret K. McElderry Books, an imprint of Simon & Schuster
ISBN: 0689839014

Having heard about Thanksgiving in school, nine-year-old Rivka tries to convince her immigrant family and her Rabbi that it is a holiday for all Americans, Jews and non-Jews alike.

Older Readers

Sigmund Freud: Pioneer of the Mind by Catherine Reef.
Clarion Books
ISBN: 0618017623

A biography of Sigmund Freud explains the methods he used to treat the mentally ill which led to the birth of psychoanalysis, and explores his controversial theories connecting dreams, desires, and behavior.

Honor Books

Younger Readers

No books were recognized in this category in 2001.

Older Readers

No books were recognized in this category in 2001.

Notable Books

Younger Readers

Behold the Trees by Sue Alexander.
Illustrations by Leonid Gore.
Arthur A. Levine, an imprint of Scholastic
ISBN: 0590762117

Recalling the history of *Eretz Yisrael* from Canaanite times to the founding of the modern state, this beautifully designed book has splendid illustrations that mirror the rise, trials, and achievements of the Jewish people as reflected by Israel's trees.

Solomon and the Trees by Matt Biers-Ariel.
Illustrations by Esti Silverberg-Kiss.
UAHC
ISBN: 0807407496

Drawing from legends about King Solomon and Jewish teachings about humankind's responsibility to care for nature, this serious, dramatically illustrated story stresses personal responsibility.

The God around Us, Volume 2: The Valley of Blessings by Mira Pollak Brichto.
Illustrations by Selina Alko.
UAHC
ISBN: 0807407380

Prayers and blessings for many of the events that occur in the lives of young children are presented in Hebrew, transliteration, and English, accompanied by lively multicultural illustrations.

Hanukkah Cat by Chaya Burstein. (Revised Edition)
Illustrations by Judy Hanks-Henn.
Kar-Ben Publishing
ISBN: 1580130291

Amusing new illustrations add sparkle to this appealing story of a little boy who finds a kitten at the start of Hanukkah. The story of the Maccabees and Lenny's adventures with the mischievous kitten are deftly interwoven.

Snow in Jerusalem by Deborah da Costa.
Illustrations by Cornelius Van Wright and Ying-Hwa Hu.
Albert Whitman
ISBN: 0807575216

During a rare day of snow in Jerusalem, a Jewish boy and an Arab boy who live in the Old City experience a rare moment of friendship when they put aside their differences to help a stray cat. Ethereal watercolor and pencil drawings portray the earthly and heavenly Jerusalem.

The Rabbi Who Flew by Renate Dollinger.
Booksmythe
ISBN: 0945585209

Colorful gouache paintings in the author-illustrator's primitive style decorate this story about a saintly rabbi with holes in his shoes. The plot expresses the mitzvah of Jew helping Jew within an idealized *shtetl* setting.

On Shabbat by Cathy Goldberg Fishman.
Illustrations by Melanie W. Hall.
Atheneum Books for Young Readers
ISBN: 0689838948

A holiday book, part of a series that is both stylish and steeped in Jewish knowledge. The dreamy illustrations capture the spirit of the Sabbath.

A Mountain of Blintzes by Barbara Diamond Goldin.
Illustrations by Anik McGrory.
Gulliver, an imprint of Harcourt Books
ISBN: 0152019022

In this humorous story of Jewish life in New York State's Catskill Mountains resort region in the 1920's, a poor family finds a way to celebrate Shavuot. The characters and action recall the traditional tales of Chelm.

The Friday Nights of Nana by Amy Hest.
Illustrations by Claire Nivola.
Candlewick Press, 2001
ISBN: 0763606588

In this serene picture book, a little girl helps her grandmother prepare for Shabbat. The celebration of tradition provides an atmosphere of closeness and warmth, a contrast to the wintry world outside.

The Hardest Word: A Yom Kippur Story by Jacqueline Jules.
Illustrations by Katherine Janus Kahn.
Kar-Ben Publishing
ISBN: 1580130305

The Ziz, a giant bird from Jewish legend, is a softy at heart. He confesses to accidentally doing wrong and God assigns him a penance: to find the hardest word. The quest is a joyful learning experience.

Zigazak! A Magical Hanukkah Night by Eric A. Kimmel.
Illustrations by Jon Goodell.
Doubleday, an imprint of Random House
ISBN: 0385326521

A pair of devils make mischief in the *shtetl* of Brisk, but the rabbi puts an end to their escapades. This jolly story transmits the traditional message that sparks of holiness can be found in unlikely places.

Cain and Abel: Finding the Fruits of Peace by Sandy Sasso.
Illustrations by Joani Keller Rothenberg.
Jewish Lights Publishing
ISBN: 1580231233

Bold splashes of color illustrate this interpretation of a Bible story that emphasizes the destructive power of anger. Running through the narrative is the midrashic tradition of nature's mourning for Abel.

The Shabbat Box by Lesley Simpson.
Illustrations by Nicole in den Bosch.
Kar-Ben Publishing
ISBN: 1580130275

When Ira loses his class's treasured Shabbat box, he solves the problem by making a new one, all on his own. This empowering story portrays a loving family, a multicultural preschool class, and a child with imagination and perseverance. Instructions for making a Shabbat box are included.

Lemuel, the Fool by Myron Uhlberg.
Illustrations by Sonja Lamut.
Peachtree Publishers
ISBN: 1561452203

Lemuel sails off in search of the city of his dreams, returns home without realizing it, and is astonished that all the people and places look so familiar! A droll, gentle story, beautifully illustrated.

Rachel Captures the Moon by Richard Ungar.
Tundra Books
ISBN: 088776505X

The foolish folk of Chelm, not content to wait for the moon to rise each evening, try to capture its luminescence permanently. When neither a ladder, nor a net, nor delicious smelling soup can lure the moon down to earth, a little girl named Rachel captures its reflection in a barrel of water.

Older Readers

Daughter of Light by Martha Attema.
Orca Book Publishers
ISBN: 1551431793

During the harsh winter of 1944, when food is scarce and electricity has been turned off, a nine-year-old Dutch girl whose mother is pregnant confronts the town's Nazi collaborationist mayor to try to convince him to restore the electricity before the baby is born.

Hans and Sophie Scholl: German Resisters of the White Rose by Toby Axelrod. (Holocaust Biography Series)
Rosen Publishing
ISBN: 0825933164

A factual account of a small group of courageous German students who resisted Hitler. Photographs, documents, a glossary, bibliography and index increase the book's value for research and reports.

Death on Sacred Ground by Harriet Feder.
Lerner Publishing
ISBN: 0822507412

She's back! Vivi Hartman, rabbi's daughter and teenage sleuth, uses Talmudic reasoning to solve a crime committed on the Seneca Reservation in New York State.

Clara's War by Kathy Kacer.
Second Story Press
ISBN: 1896764428

Thirteen-year-old Clara and her family are deported from Prague to the concentration camp of Terezin. Through their experiences, the grimness and terror of the camp are shown in contrast to its rich cultural life.

Rivka's Way by Teri Kanefield.
Front Street, an imprint of Cricket Books
ISBN: 0812628705

Set in eighteenth century Prague, this tells of teenage Rivka's longing to leave the safety of the Jewish Quarter and venture into the larger world that fascinates her outside.

Understanding Buddy by Mark Kornblatt.
Margaret K. McElderry Books, an imprint of Simon & Schuster
ISBN: 0668983215X

A fifth grader discovers that the withdrawn, silent new boy in class is grieving over the sudden death of his mother. Rebuffed by Buddy when he tries to be friendly, Sam searches for answers, including Jewish answers, to the disturbing questions that arise as he tries to understand Buddy.

Stolen Words by Amy Koss.
American Girl
ISBN: 1584853778

Everything is going wrong on Robyn's vacation with her family in Austria! As recorded in her diary., Robyn's comments and observations are filled with both biting teenage wit and deep concern about her mother, who cannot get over the death of her sister. A colloquial style imparts a serious theme.

Daughter of Fire: Heroines of the Bible by Fran Manushkin.
Illustrations by Uri Shulevitz.
Silver Whistle, an imprint of Harcourt
ISBN: 0152018697

Drawing on both the Bible and on legend, the author portrays heroines of passion and purpose, representing Jewish history from the period of the Patriarchs to the Persian era.

The War Within by Carol Matas.
Simon & Schuster
ISBN: 0689829353

After General Grant issues an order expelling all Jews from the territory under his control, teenaged Hannah Green, a Southern belle in the making, begins to question many of the values she took for granted, including slavery.

Secrets in the House of Delgado by Gloria Miklowitz.
Eerdmanns
ISBN: 0802852068

In a gripping story about "New Christians" and the Inquisition, the author captures the terror of the times and the varying degrees of Jewish loyalty among members of one family.

Shoes for Amelie by Connie Steiner.
Illustrations by Denis Rodier.
Lobster Press
ISBN: 1894222377

The heroism of the people of the town of Le Chambon-sur-Lignon, France is portrayed through a story about one courageous and "ordinary" family who sheltered a Jewish child during the Holocaust.

Friend of Foe? By Eva Vogiel.
Judaica Press
ISBN: 188058266X

The headmistress of an Orthodox boarding school for girls in England is anxious to discover who, among the school's neighbors, seems to be trying to close it down. Likeable characters and an engrossing plot convey a theme of tolerance.

Surviving Hitler: A Boy in the Nazi Death Camps by Andrea Warren.
HarperCollins
ISBN: 0688174973

An inspiring account of the Holocaust experiences of Jack Mandelbaum, who survived three years as a teen in several camps. His zest for life and ability to form friendships enabled him to begin a new life in the United States.

Mendel Rosenbusch: Tales for Jewish Children by Ilse Weber
Translated by Ruth and Hans Fisher.
Herodias
ISBN: 1928746195

Mendel is a good and wise man who has been granted the power to become invisible. He uses his gift to help the poor and right wrongs. These tales paint a knowing portrait of small town life and culture in pre-Holocaust Central Europe.

The Magic Menorah: A Modern Chanukah Tale by Jane Breskin Zalben.
Illustrations by Donna Diamond.
Simon & Schuster
ISBN: 06898226060

An encounter with a Yiddish-spouting genie named Fishel changes Stanley's mind about Hanukkah and family traditions.

Teen Readers

After the Holocaust by Howard Greenfeld.
Greenwillow Books
ISBN: 0688177552

Focusing on eight Holocaust survivors now living in the United States, this powerful book shows the hardships faced by young survivors, many of whom were without homes, families, identities or hope.

Mara's Stories: Glimmers in the Dark by Gary Schmidt.
Henry Holt
ISBN: 0805067949

In the night and fog of a concentration camp, women and children gather at night to listen to stories told by a prisoner named Mara, the daughter of a rabbi. The stories are adapted from Jewish lore; the listening is an act of resistance.

2000 Awards

Younger Readers

Gershon's Monster: A Story for The Jewish New Year by Eric A. Kimmel.
Illustrations by Jon J. Muth.
Scholastic Press
ISBN: 043910839X

When his sins threaten the lives of his beloved twin children, a Jewish man finally repents of his wicked ways.

Older Readers

The Key Is Lost by Ida Vos.
Translated by Terese Edelstein.
Morrow, an imprint of HarperCollins
ISBN: 0688162835

Based on a true story, this historical fiction tells of two young sisters who get separated from their parents and are forced to live hidden away in the attics of Holland in order to escape from being caught by the Nazis.

Honor Books

Younger Readers

The Market Wedding by Cary Fagan.
Illustrations by Regolo Ricci.
Tundra Books of Northern New York
ISBN: 0887764924

A fishmonger falls in love with the milliner whose cart is across the street from his in the turn-of-the-century Kensington Market, and even though his plan for a fine wedding backfires, all ends well.

The Wisdom Bird: a Tale of Solomon and Sheba by Sheldon Oberman.
Illustrations by Neil Waldman.
Boyds Mills Press
ISBN: 1563978164

When the Queen of Sheba, the wisest woman in the world, comes to Jerusalem to present an unusual request to King Solomon, the wisest man in the world, the fate of every bird in the world is at stake.

Older Readers

Love You, Soldier by Amy Hest.
Illustrations by Sonja Lamut.
Candlewick Press
ISBN: 0763609439

Katie, a Jewish girl living in New York City during World War II, sees many dynamic changes in her world as she ages from seven to ten waiting for her father to return from the war.

Fireflies in the Dark: The Story of Friedl Dicker-Brandeis and the Children of Terezin by Susan Goldman Rubin.
Holiday House
ISBN: 082341681X

Recounts how Friedl Dicker, a Jewish woman from Czechoslovakia, taught art to children at the Terezin Concentration Camp.

The Legend of Freedom Hill by Linda Jacobs Altman.
Illustrations by Cornelius Van Wright and Ying-Hwa Hu.
Lee and Low
ISBN: 1584300035

California in the Gold Rush era is the setting for this heartwarming story of an inter-racial relationship. Two little girls, one Jewish and one African-American, find enough gold to ransom the runaways the slave catcher has in his clutches. Colorful, realistic illustrations reflect the setting, characters, and drama.

On Purim by Cathy Goldberg Fishman.
Illustrations by Melanie W. Hall.
Atheneum Books for Young Readers
ISBN: 0689823924

One of the best of the books on holidays created by Fishman and Hall, this combines evocative illustrations with a narrative that is sensitive to the paradoxes of a holiday in which God's name is never mentioned.

Dance, Sing, Remember by Leslie Kimmelman.
Illustrations by Ora Eitan.
HarperCollins
ISBN: 0060277254

A light-hearted writing style and child-like illustrations give panache to this cheerful holiday collection.

Come, Let Us Be Joyful: The Story of Hava Nagila by Fran Manushkin.
Illustrations by Rosalind Charney Kaye.
UAHC
ISBN: 0807407313

Children who have sung and danced to "*Hava Nagila*" will learn how it may have come to be transformed from a sad Yiddish melody to the musical embodiment of pioneering Zionism. An ebulliently written and illustrated story set in Israel before statehood.

Moishe's Miracle by Laura Kraus Melmed.
Illustrations by David Slonim.
HarperCollins
ISBN: 0688146821

One the eve of Hanukkah, a poor man receives a magic frying pan that produces endless latkes. Moishe wants to feed the whole village but his wife, Baila, has other ideas... The deep, dusky pictures glow with magic.

Thread of Kindness: A Tzedaka Story by Leah Shollar.
Illustrations by Shoshana Mekibel.
HaChai Publishing
ISBN: 1929628013

Goodness rewarded is the theme of this traditional story about a poor family who use the six years of plenty given to them by Elijah to help others. The message is conveyed gently and illustrated with soft pastels.

Older Readers

Samir and Yonatan by Daniella Carmi.
Translated by Yael Lotan.
Arthur A. Levine, an imprint of Scholastic
ISBN: 0439135044

Frightened to be the only Palestinian in the children's ward of a hospital in Israel, Samir withdraws into himself. Gradually, Yonatan, the boy in the next bed, draws him into another world where Jews and Palestinians can be friends. (Mildred L. Batchelder Award Winner)

The Yellow Star: The Legend of King Christian X of Denmark by Carmen Agra Deedy.
Illustrations by Henry Sorensen.
Peachtree Publishers
ISBN: 1561452084

A beautifully illustrated tribute to the tolerance of the Danish People and their king, who took many risks on behalf of the Jewish population during the German occupation of World War II.

Photo Odyssey: Solomon Carvalho's Remarkable Western Adventure, 1853-1854 by Arlene B. Kirschfelder.
Clarion Books
ISBN: 0339589123X

Carvalho, a Baltimore Jew of Sephardic ancestry, was a tenderfoot when he joined an expedition led by the explorer John Charles Fremont. This well-researched biography gives a stirring account of his adventure.

Torn Thread by Ann Isaacs.
Scholastic
ISBN: 0590603639

Based on the experiences of a Holocaust survivor, this is the story of two teenaged sisters who survive a Nazi slave labor camp where they were imprisoned for several years. Through a large cast of characters, the author touches on some central Holocaust issues.

Tales for the Seventh Day by Nina Jaffe.
Illustrations by Kelly Stribling Sutherland.
Scholastic
ISBN: 0590120549

Seven tales follow a gracefully written introduction describing traditional observances that have maintained Jewish identity and continuity. The tales are adapted from Talmud, folk literature, and oral traditions.

The Jar of Fools: Eight Hanukkah Stories from Chelm by Eric A. Kimmel.
Illustrations by Mordicai Gerstein.
Holiday House
ISBN: 0823414639

Too delicious to be enjoyed only at Hanukkah, these effervescent tales show how the wisdom of fools might be the wisest kind of all!

Pharaoh's Daughter by Julius Lester.
Silver Whistle, an imprint of Harcourt
ISBN: 0152018265

A dazzling portrait of ancient Egypt and a provocative story of religious and cultural identity are created in this free interpretation of the youth of Moses and his older sister.

Darkness over Denmark: The Danish Resistance and the Rescue of the Jews by Ellen Levine.
Holiday House
ISBN: 0823414477

Interviews with individuals involved in the Danish resistance, documentary photographs, and a lucid text combine to tell an inspiring true story.

Hannah's Journal: The Story of an Immigrant Girl by Marissa Moss. (Young American Voices Series)
Silver Whistle, an imprint of Harcourt
ISBN: 0152021558

The exciting story of Hannah's trip from Russia to America is told through her journal entries. The format, with lined pages, hand lettering, and Hannah's drawings and comments in the margins, is especially appealing.

Why on This Night? A Passover Haggadah for Family Celebration by Rahel Musleah.
Illustrations by Louise August.
Simon & Schuster Books for Young Readers
ISBN: 088776519X

Intended to give children a central part in planning and participating in the Passover Seder, this includes every major part of the *Haggadah* in Hebrew, English and transliteration. And, as if that weren't enough, there are also superb illustrations, songs, games, crafts, recipes, and other ideas for making the Seder truly family-centered.

The Butterfly by Patricia Polacco.
Philomel Books
ISBN: 0399231706

During the Nazi occupation of France, a child discovers that her mother is hiding Jews. The "little ghost" who appears in her bedroom at night is one of them. Monique and Sevrine become friends, sharing hope for a brighter future symbolized by the butterfly. A poignant story whose illustrations (by the author) express its mood.

Escaping to America: A True Story by Rosalind Schanzer.
HarperCollins
ISBN: 0688169899

In the early twentieth century, a family of Polish Jews, headed by a determined father, leaves the Old Country. This book, vibrantly illustrated (by the author), expresses their thankfulness and pride in becoming Americans.

The Day the Rabbi Disappeared: Jewish Holiday Tales of Magic by Howard Schwartz.
Illustrations by Monique Passicot.
Viking
ISBN: 0670887331

The magic in these tales -- of dreams, heavenly journeys, and secret names -- is used to protect and save the Jewish people. Several of the stories feature learned women and all twelve of them are associated with the major festivals, Rosh Chodesh, and Shabbat.

My Secret Camera: Life in the Lodz Ghetto by Frank Dabba Smith.
Photographs by Mendel Grossman.
Gulliver, an imprint of Harcourt
ISBN: 0152023062

Mendel Grossman did not survive the Holocaust, but his photographs did. They are heartbreaking reminders of everyday life in a community destined for destruction.

***Faraway Home* by Marilyn Taylor.**
O'Brien Press (Ireland - 1999)
ISBN: 0531145247

An Austrian brother and sister are sent on the *Kindertransport* to Northern Ireland, where a farm for Jewish refugees from Hilter was established near Belfast. Actual events are integrated with sympathetic characters, believable relationships, well-paced action, and a portrayal of lives forever changed by war.

***Invisible Chains* by Eva Vogiel.**
Judaica Press
ISBN: 1880582570

An Orthodox boarding school in England is the setting for this story of two sisters. A wise headmistress and a concerned young teacher intervene to solve the girls' potentially destructive relationship. Traditional Judaism guides and supports all of them.

***Remember Me: A Search for Refuge in Wartime Britain* by Irene N. Watts.**
Tundra Books
ISBN: 088776519X

Twelve-year-old Marianne, who was introduced in *Goodbye, Marianne* (Tunda, 1998), is sent on the *Kindertransport* to England. Missing her parents and yearning for the familiarity of Jewish family life, she struggles in a series of foster homes. A fascinating picture of war-time England -- of courage and narrow social attitudes -- is painted.

1999 Awards

Younger Readers

The Peddler's Gift **by Maxine Schur.**
Illustrations by Kimberly Bulcken Root.
Dial Books for Young Readers
ISBN: 080371987

A young boy in turn-of-the-century rural Russia learns that appearances are often deceiving after he steals and then tries to return a dreidel to the traveling peddler Shnook.

Older Readers

Speed of Light **by Sybil Rosen.**
Anne Schwartz Books, an imprint of Atheneum Books for Young Readers
ISBN: 0689841515

An eleven-year-old Jewish girl living in the South during the 1950s struggles with the anti-Semitism and racism which pervade her small community.

Honor Books

Younger Readers

Noah and the Great Flood **by Mordicai Gerstein.**
Simon & Schuster Books for Young Readers
ISBN: 0689813716

A retelling of the biblical story of how Noah and his family were saved, along with two of every living creature, when God destroyed the wicked of the world with a devastating flood.

Joseph Had a Little Overcoat **by Simms Taback.**
Viking Children's Books
ISBN: 0670878553

An old Eastern European folk song provides the basis for a tale about a peasant who devises clever uses for his worn-out overcoat.

Baby's Bris by Susan Wilkowski.
Illustrations by Judith Friedman.
Kar-Ben Publishing
ISBN: 1580130534

Sophie becomes a big sisterand, during the first eight days of her brother s life, learns about the custom of *bris* (circumcision) and celebrates the event with her family and new brother Ben.

Older Readers

Journeys with Elijah by Barbara Diamond Goldin.
Illustrations by Jerry Pinkney
Gulliver, an imprint of Harcourt Brace & Company
ISBN: 0152004459

Presents eight stories about the biblical prophet Elijah set in a variety of time periods and in places all over the world where Jews have lived.

When The Beginning Began: Stories About God, the Creatures and Us by **Julius Lester.**
Illustrations by Emily Lisker.
Silver Whistle, an imprint of Harcourt Brace & Company
ISBN: 0152012389

A collection of traditional and original Jewish tales interpreting the Biblical story of the creation of the world.

When the Soldiers Were Gone by Vera Propp.
G.P. Putnam's Sons
ISBN: 0698118812

After the German occupation of the Netherlands, Benjamin leaves the Christian family with whom he had been living and is reunited with his real Jewish parents who returned from hiding and whom Benjamin doesn't remember.

Notable Books

Younger Readers

David and the Trash-Talkin' Giant: Mr. Grungy's Seek and Find Bible Stories by Joel Anderson.
Illustrations by Abe Goolsby.
Tommy Nelson
ISBN: 0849959187

The story of David and Goliath is retold in rhyme with clever illustrations of scrap creations that have been digitally photographed.

Queen Esther, the Morning Star by **Mordicai Gerstein.**
Simon & Schuster Books for Young Readers
ISBN: 0689813724

A highly sophisticated interpretation of tradition. A visual treat and atmospherically a Jewish *Arabian Nights.*

How Yussel Caught the Gefilte Fish: A Shabbos Story by **Charlotte Herman.**
Illustrations by Katya Krenina.
Dutton Children's Books
ISBN: 0525454497

When Yussel goes fishing with his father, it's both a bonding experience and an opportunity to bring home his favorite treat.

This Is Our Seder by **Ziporah Hildebrandt.**
Illustrations by Robin Roraback.
Holiday House
ISBN: 0823414361

This title, which is organized around the themes of continuity and extended family, presents events and symbolic activities associated with Passover.

The Lion and the Unicorn by **Shirley Hughes.**
DK Publishing
ISBN: 07899425556

When Lenny Levi is evacuated from World War II London to an aristocrat's estate, he must find the courage to conquer loneliness and the rejection that comes with being "different." Stirring illustrations of war and rural beauty.

***The Ten Commandments for Jewish Children* by Miriam Nerlove.**
Albert Whitman
ISBN: 0807577707

A traditional approach in clear language. The author emphasizes the contemporary validity of these ancient teachings and suggests how they may be put into practice.

***The Very Best Hanukkah Gift* by Joanne Rocklin.**
Illustrations by Catherine O'Neil.
Delacorte Press, an imprint of Random House
ISBN: 0385326564

Daniel, an awkward eight-year-old middle child, anticipates Hanukkah with anxiety, but unexpected events bolster his self-esteem and his status within the family.

***Matzah Ball Soup* by Joan Rothenberg.**
Hyperion Books for Children
ISBN: 0786821701

The humble matzah ball is the vehicle of transmission of Jewish tradition from generation to generation.

***For Heaven's Sake* by Sandy Sasso.**
Illustrations by Karyn Kunz Finney.
Jewish Lights Publishing
ISBN: 1580230547

A young boy grieving for this much-loved grandfather seeks to understand the concept of heaven.

***Raisel's Riddle* by Erica Silverman.**
Illustrations by Susan Gaber.
Farrar Straus and Giroux
ISBN: 0374351681

A Jewish orphan girl finds happiness with her "prince," a rabbi's son who appreciates her learning as well as her beauty.

Streets of Gold **by Rosemary Wells.**
Illustrations by Dann Andreasen.
Dial Books for Young Readers
ISBN: 0803721498

Based on Mary Antin's classic immigration memoir, *The Promised Land* (1912), this story describes a young girl's adaptation to American life and her love for her adopted country.

King Solomon and His Magic Ring **by Elie Wiesel.**
Illustrations by Mark Podwal.
Greenwillow Books
ISBN: 0688169597

A collection of wonder tales, based on Talmud and Midrash, featuring angels, demons, flying carpets, and conversations with animals.

The Memory Coat **by Elvira Woodruff.**
Illustrations by Michael Dooling.
Scholastic
ISBN: 0590677179

Rachel saves the day when it appears that her cousin, Grisha, will fail the health examination at Ellis Island and be sent back to Russia.

Older Readers

With All My Heart, With All My Mind: Thirteen Stories about Growing up Jewish **edited by Sandy Asher.**
Simon & Schuster
ISBN: 0689820127

Original stories dealing with teen identity crises by American-Jewish authors, followed by interviews. Varied and highly readable.

Two Suns in the Sky **by Miriam Bat Ami.**
Front Street, an imprint of Cricket Books
ISBN: 081269000

In 1944, in wartime Oswego, New York, two teens, a Yugoslavian Jewish refugee boy and an American Roman Catholic girl from a strict family reach out to one another. Their relationship results in sorrow and growth.

My Bridges of Hope: Searching for Life and Love after Auschwitz by Livia Bitton-Jackson.
Simon & Schuster Books for Young Readers
ISBN: 0689820267

This sequel to *I Have Lived a Thousand Years* (1997) takes Elli Friedman from liberation to her arrival in the United States six years later. As a survivor and displaced person, the heroine attempts to form relationships and continue her education, yet feels guilty for wanting a normal life.

Escape: Teens Who Escaped the Holocaust to Freedom by Sandra Giddens. (Teen Witnesses to the Holocaust Series)
Rosen Publishing Group
ISBN: 0823928438

A well-written account of four teens who survived due to courage, luck, and the assistance of others. All went on to lead productive lives and build new families.

Miriam by Beatrice Gormley.
Eerdmans Books for Young Readers
ISBN: 0802851568

Moses' sister leader of her people, faced with all the temptations to assimilate that ancient Egypt had to offer.

Running on Eggs by Anna Levine.
Front Street, an imprint of Cricket Books
ISBN: 0812628756

A tentative friendship develops between an Israeli girl from a kibbutz and an Arab girl from a nearby village when both become members of a track team.

The Cure by Sonia Levitin.
Harcourt Brace & Company
ISBN: 152018271

A stunning work that moves in time from a sterile future civilization to the rich but dangerous world of medieval Jewry and back.

My Name Is Not Gussie by Mikki Machlin.
Houghton Mifflin
ISBN: 0395956463

A high-spirited girl experiences the trials and joys of immigrant life.

The Good Liar by Gregory Maguire.
Clarion Books
ISBN: 0395906970

To the dismay of their devout and gentle mother, three French brothers delight in telling outrageous lies. When Jews are hidden in their village after the fall of Paris, lying is no longer a game.

In My Enemy's House by Carol Matas.
Simon & Schuster Books for Young Readers
ISBN: 0689813546

Marissa, a fifteen-year-old Jewish girl, poses as a Roman Catholic worker in wartime Germany. She makes her way in a world of random cruelty, a world that imposes terrible choices.

Missing Girls by Lois Metzger.
Viking
ISBN: 0670877778

After her mother's death, Carrie's father sends her to live with her Holocaust survivor grandmother. Slowly, the teenager begins to recapture her engagement with life and other people.

A Coat for the Moon and Other Jewish Tales edited by Howard Schwartz and Barbara Rush.
Illustrations by Michael Iofin.
Jewish Publication Society
ISBN: 082760596X

A fine collection, often subtle. Beautifully illustrated.

Einstein: Visionary Scientist by John Severance.
Clarion Books
ISBN: 0395931002

A readable account for Einstein's momentous scientific discoveries and his often troubled personal life.

Star of Luís by Marc Talbert.
Clarion Books
ISBN: 039591423X

A Hispanic boy, raised as a Roman Catholic, struggles to understand and to be reconciled with his newly discovered Iberian-Jewish ancestry.

1998 Awards

Younger Readers

Nine Spoons **by Marci Stillerman.**
Illustrations by Pesach Gerber.
HaChai Publishing
ISBN: 0922613842

A few brave souls in a Nazi camp are determined to gather nine spoons to make a menorah for Chanukah.

Older Readers

Stones in Water **by Donna Jo Napoli.**
Dutton Books
ISBN: 0141306009

After being taken by German soldiers from a local movie theater along with other Italian boys including his Jewish friend, Roberto is forced to work in Germany, escapes into the Ukrainian winter, before desperately trying to make his way back home to Venice.

Honor Books

Younger Readers

Queen Esther Saves Her People **by Rita Golden Gelman.**
Illustrations by Frane Lessac.
Scholastic
ISBN: 0590470256

Retells the story of how a beautiful Jewish girl became the Queen of Persia and saved her people from death at the hands of the evil Haman.

You Never Know: A Legend of the Lamed-Vavniks **by Francine Prose.**
Illustrations by Mark Podwal.
Greenwillow Books
ISBN: 0688157580

Though mocked by the rest of the villagers, poor Schmuel the shoemaker turns out to be a very special person.

On the Wings of Eagles: An Ethiopian Boy's Story **by Jeffrey Schrier.**
Millbrook Press
ISBN: 076130004X

A Jewish Ethiopian boy recounts the story of Israel's 1991 airlift rescue of his threatened people.

The Magic of Kol Nidre **by Bruce Siegel.**
Illustrations by Shelly O. Haas.
Kar-Ben Publishing
ISBN: 158013002X

The magic of the Kol Nidre prayer, central to the Yom Kippur service, is explored from the viewpoint of three generations.

Older Readers

The Treasure in the Tiny Blue Tin **by Dede Fox Ducharme.**
Texas Christian University Press
ISBN: 0875651801

In the early 1900's in Texas, a twelve-year-old Jewish immigrant runs away to search for his father who he fears is sick, and he is joined on his dangerous journey by a prejudiced country boy.

The Singing Mountain **by Sonia Levitin.**
Simon & Schuster Books for Young Readers
ISBN: 068983523X

While traveling in Israel for the summer, seventeen-year-old Mitch decides to stay and pursue a life of Jewish orthodoxy, forcing him to make some important decisions about the family and life he is leaving in southern California.

No Pretty Pictures: A Child of War by Anita Lobel.
Greenwillow Books
ISBN: 0380732858

The author describes her experiences as a Polish Jew during World War II and for years in Sweden afterwards.

Notable Books

Younger Readers

Agnon's Alef Bet: Poems by S. Y. Agnon.
Translated by Robert Friend.
Illustrations by Arieh Zeldich.
Jewish Publication Society
ISBN: 0827605994

Playful illustrations match each of these poems inspired by the letters of the Hebrew alphabet and written by the Nobel Prize winning Israeli writer. The original Hebrew versions are included.

Journey to Ellis Island: How My Father Came to America by Carol Bierman with Barbara Hehner.
Illustrations by Laurie McGaw.
Hyperion Books for Children
ISBN: 0786803770

An effective combination of documentary photographs, postcards, and realistic sepia-tone illustrations highlight this engrossing true story, based on the experiences of the author's father.

The Way Meat Loves Salt by Nina Jaffe.
Illustrations by Louise August.
Henry Holt
ISBN: 080504043845

Charming to the eye and ear, this Jewish version of the Cinderella story is stunningly illustrated and perfect for shared reading.

Noah's Ark by Heinz Janisch.
Illustrations by Lisbeth Zwerger.
Translated by Rosemary Lanning.
North-South Books
ISBN: 1558587845

A new perspective on an oft-told tale is given by slightly surreal illustrations that show sunken towns from underwater and mythical as well as human figures scurrying for higher ground.

Once Upon a Shabbos by Jacqueline Jules.
Illustrations by Katherine Janus Kahn.
Kar-Ben Publishing
ISBN: 1580130208

Whether or not readers are familiar with a variant of this story called "Sody Sallyratus," they are sure to be captivated by this Yiddish-flavored version, set in New York, featuring a lost bear and a resourceful *bubbe*.

One More Border by William Kaplan with Shelley Tanaka.
Illustrations by Stephen Taylor.
Douglas & McIntyre
ISBN: 0888993323

Fans of fiction and non-fiction will both enjoy this suspenseful memoir of a family's escape from war-ravaged Europe during World War II.

When Mindy Saved Hanukkah by Eric A. Kimmel.
Illustrations by Barbara McClintock.
Scholastic
ISBN: 0590371363

New York's historic Eldridge Street *shul* is the setting for a winsome story about a family of little people, akin to the Borrowers, who live within its walls. Illustrations and book design impart Victorian charm.

Miriam's Cup by Fran Manushkin.
Illustrations by Bob Dacey.
Scholastic
ISBN: 0590677209

Vivid illustrations enhance this story about Miriam, which draws on Biblical, *Midrashic*, and modern feminist sources.

The Menorah Story by Mark Podwal.
Greenwillow Books
ISBN: 0688157580

A clearly written account of the two menorahs of Jewish tradition, enhanced by deeply colored, symbolic illustrations (by the author).

The Kugel Valley Klezmer Band by Joan Betty Stuchner.
Illustrations by Richard Row.
North Winds Press
ISBN: 0590038338

In a Canadian village around the turn of the century, Shira learns to play the fiddle and realizes her dream of performing with the klezmer band.

In Our Image: God's First Creatures by Nancy Sohn Swartz.
Illustrations by Melanie Hall.
Jewish Lights Publishing
ISBN: 1879045990

Each of the creatures that the Almighty created is asked to share its special gift with humankind, the last to be brought into the world.

Annushka's Voyage by Edith Tarbescu.
Illustrations by Lydia Dabcovich.
Clarion Books
ISBN: 039564366X

Two little girls leave their village in Russia to take an arduous and adventure-filled voyage aboard a steamship to join their papa in New York.

Older Readers

Clouds of Glory by Miriam Chaikin.
Illustrations by David Frampton.
Clarion Books
ISBN: 039574654X

Vibrant woodcuts illustrate legends from the Bible based on traditional and modern *Midrash*.

Faraway Summer by Johanna Hurwitz.
Illustrations by Mary Azarian.
Morrow Junior Books
ISBN: 0688153348

In the summer of 1910, a Jewish girl from the teeming streets of New York City spends two weeks with a Vermont farm family -- an experience that changes all of them.

A Hanukkah Treasury by Eric A. Kimmel.
Illustrations by Emily Lisker.
Henry Holt
ISBN: 0805052933

Information, stories, poetry, and sprightly illustrations distinguish this outstanding collection.

The Storyteller's Beads by Jane Kurtz.
Harcourt Brace
ISBN: 0152010742

A blind Jewish girl and a Christian girl overcome prejudice and suspicion as they help one another on a hazardous exodus from Ethiopia to a refugee camp in the Sudan.

Dreams of the Golden Country: The Diary of Zipporah Feldman, a Jewish Immigrant Girl by Kathryn Lasky.
Scholastic Press
ISBN: 0590029738

Part of the popular "Dear America" series, this engaging story captures the emotions, experiences, and aspirations of an immigrant girl as she records them in her diary.

Greater Than Angels by Carol Matas.
Simon & Schuster Books for Young Readers
ISBN: 0689813538
A courageous teenage heroine joins the righteous gentiles of Le Chambon sur Lignon, France in resisting the Nazis and smuggling her fellow Jews over the border to Switzerland.

Israel: The Founding of a Modern Nation by Maida Silverman.
Illustrations by Susan Avishai.
Dial Books
ISBN: 0805721558

A very readable introduction to the people and events leading to the establishment, in 1948, of the State of Israel, after thousands of years of exile, struggle, and hope.

Masada **by Neil Waldman.**
Morrow Junior Books
ISBN: 0688144814

Looming high above the Dead Sea, the ancient fortress of Masada possessed secrets that modern archaeology helped to reveal.

Teen Readers

Walk the Dark Streets **by Edith Baer.**
Farrar Straus and Giroux
ISBN: 0374382298

A moving fictionalized chronicle of the deterioration of life for German Jews in the 1930s.

To Bigotry No Sanction: The Story of the Oldest Synagogue in America **by Leonard Everett Fisher.**
Holiday House
ISBN: 0823414019
The history of Newport, Rhode Island's Touro Synagogue sets the stage for a succinct examination of the odyssey of Sephardic Jews to North America and the development of religious liberty in the United States.

Masada: The Last Fortress **by Gloria Miklowitz.**
Eerdmans Books for Young Readers
ISBN: 0802851657

Antagonists in the Roman siege of Masada, one a teenage zealot boy and the other the Roman general leading the attack, tell their stories as the conflict progresses to its tragic conclusion.

Thanks to My Mother **by Schoschana Rabinovici.**
Translated by James Skofield.
Dial Books
ISBN: 0803722354

From the Vilna Ghetto to the camps and a death march, young Susie's survival depended on her indomitable mother.

***Katarina* by Kathryn Winter.**
Farrar Straus and Giroux
ISBN: 0374339848

Outcast and struggling, virtually alone, to survive in Slovakia during the Holocaust Katarina is sustained by a child's blend of imagination, hope, and faith in Catholic saints. A remarkable story about identity and difference.

1997 Awards

Younger Readers

***When Zaydeh Danced on Eldridge Street* by Elsa Okon Rael.**
Illustrations by Marjorie Priceman.
Simon & Schuster Books for Young Readers
ISBN: 0689804512

While staying with her grandparents in New York City in the mid-1930's, eight-year-old Zeesie joins in the celebration of *Simchat Torah* and sees a different side of her stern grandfather.

Older Readers

***The Mysterious Visitor: Stories of the Prophet Elijah* by Nina Jaffe.**
Illustrations by Elivia Savadier.
Scholastic
ISBN: 0590484222

A collection of folktales featuring the prophet Elijah, a messenger from heaven who comes to earth in many disguises.

Honor Books

Younger Readers

When Jessie Came Across the Sea by Amy Hest.
Illustrations by P.J. Lynch.
Candlewick Press
ISBN: 076361274X

A thirteen-year-old Jewish orphan reluctantly leaves her grandmother and immigrates to New York City, where she works for three years sewing lace and earning money to bring Grandmother to the United States, too.

Older Readers

I Have Lived a Thousand Years: Growing Up in the Holocaust by Livia Bitton-Jackson.
Simon & Schuster Books for Young Readers
ISBN: 0689823959

The author describes her experiences during World War II when she and her family were sent to the death camp at Auschwitz.

Notable Books

Younger Readers

On Passover by Cathy Goldberg Fishman.
Illustrations by Melanie W. Hall.
Atheneum Books for Young Readers
ISBN: 0689805284

The symbols, customs, and meaning of Passover are explained from the point of view of a young child and enhanced with attractive illustrations.

On Rosh Hashanah and Yom Kippur by Cathy Goldberg Fishman.
Illustrations by Melanie W. Hall.
Atheneum Books for Young Readers
ISBN: 0689805268

The spiritual significance of Rosh Hashanah and Yom Kippur are experienced concretely by a little girl and expressed with reverence and sincerity. Winsome illustrations extend the simple story.

Jonah and the Two Great Fish by Mordicai Gerstein.
Simon & Schuster Books for Young Readers
ISBN: 0689813732

Strands of legend embellish a fancifully illustrated version of the Bible story.

The Borrowed Hanukkah Latkes by Linda Glaser.
Illustrations by Nancy Cote.
Albert Whitman
ISBN: 0807508411

A little girl and her lonely neighbor are the focal point of this intergenerational story about kindness and sharing.

Joseph and His Coat of Many Colors by Sue Kassirer.
Illustrations by Danuta Jarecka.
Simon & Schuster Books for Young Readers
ISBN: 0689812272

Beginning readers will enjoy reading this Bible story on their own. Colorful illustrations complement the story.

Annie's Shabbat by Sarah Marwil Lamstein.
Illustrations by Cecily Lang.
Albert Whitman
ISBN: 0807503762

In six short, attractively illustrated chapters that begin with preparations for Shabbat and end with Havdalah, Annie and her family celebrate Shabbat at home, at synagogue, and with some stories from our past.

Marven of the Great North Woods by Kathryn Lasky.
Illustrations by Kevin Hawkes.
Harcourt Brace
ISBN: 0152001042

Large, evocative illustrations are a stunning backdrop to this story of a small Jewish boy and a bearish French Canadian lumberjack who become friends in a logging camp during the influenza epidemic of 1918.

***The Boat of Many Rooms* by J. Patrick Lewis.**
Illustrations by Reg Cartwright.
Atheneum Books for Young Readers
ISBN: 0689801181

Each stylized, large-eyed figure, whether human or animal, is sharply defined and distinctively composed upon the pages of this somewhat unusual Noah story, written in several styles of verse.

***Elisabeth* by Claire Nivola.**
Farrar Straus and Giroux
ISBN: 0374320853

Years after fleeing from the Nazis, a young woman is reunited with the beloved doll she left behind in Germany. The writing style and illustrations are elegant, restrained, and moving.

***By the Hanukkah Light* by Sheldon Oberman.**
Illustrations by Neil Waldman.
Boyds Mills Press
ISBN: 1563976587

Parallels between ancient and modern Jewish history are shown in a story celebrating religious freedom through the primary symbol of a family menorah that survived the Holocaust. A warm tone suffuses hope into cold history.

***The Angel's Mistake: Stories of Chelm* by Francine Prose.**
Illustrations by Marc Podwal.
Greenwillow Books
ISBN: 0688149057

In a charming marriage of words and pictures, this version of some of the Chelm stories, adapted successfully for a younger than usual audience, tells of how a botched mission by two angels created Chelm, the town of fools.

***Purim Play* by Roni Schotter.**
Illustrations by Marilyn Hafner.
Little Brown
ISBN: 0316775185

By means of a play rehearsal, the story of Purim is filtered through the personalities and perspectives of several children and their reaction to an elderly neighbor asked to play Haman. Rollicking illustrations.

In My Pocket by Dorrith M. Sim.
Illustrations by Gerald Fitzgerald.
Harcourt Brace
ISBN: 0152013571

On a morning in July 1939, a young Jewish child sails from Holland to the safety of a new life in Scotland. A simply told, strikingly illustrated story of the Kindertransport.

The Never-Ending Greenness by Neil Waldman.
Morrow Junior Books
ISBN: 0688133799

A Tu B'Shvat story set in Israel, this tenderly tells of building a new life and a new land through the mitzvah of planting trees. The pointillist-style illustrations are stunning.

The Two Brothers: A Legend of Jerusalem by Neil Waldman.
Atheneum Books for Young Readers
ISBN: 0689319363

A new version of a beloved Talmudic legend about loving-kindness, each page awash in softly colored, highly textured illustrations that are reminiscent of ancient frescoes.

Joseph by Brian Wildsmith.
W.B. Eerdmans
ISBN: 0802851614

No wonder the wandering Israelites longed for the fleshpots of Egypt if it looked as glorious as it does in Wildsmith's intensely colored and richly detailed illustrations.

Pearl's Marigolds for Grandpa by Jane Breskin Zalben.
Simon & Schuster Books for Young Readers
ISBN: 0689804482

The pain of loss and the solace of memory are expressed in this warm story about the death of Pearl's grandpa. Small, delicate illustrations with floral motifs are appealing.

Older Readers

Two Cents and a Milk Bottle by Lee Cha'ah Batterman.
Illustrations by James Wattling.
Alef Design
ISBN: 11881283178

Strong Jewish identity and positive Jewish values underscore this nostalgic story of first generation Americans in a New York immigrant neighborhood set in the 1930s.

The Dead Sea Scrolls by **Ilene Cooper.**
Illustrations by John Thompson.
Morrow Junior Books
ISBN: 0688143008

Few archaeological finds can match the discovery of the Dead Sea Scrolls for drama and controversy. These elements are treated thoroughly, accurately and fairly in this excellent account that includes reference aids.

The Broken Mirror: A Novella by **Kirk Douglas.**
Simon & Schuster Books for Young Readers
ISBN: 0689814933

This short, absorbing novel deals with the loss of faith and its recovery in the aftermath of the Holocaust.

Memories of Anne Frank: Reflections of a Childhood Friend by **Alison Leslie Gold.**
Scholastic
ISBN: 0590907220

The clipped style of this double Holocaust memoir, that of the famous Anne and her unknown friend, Hannah, will keep readers absorbed and eager to see what happens to Hannah as well as to learn more about Anne.

While the Candles Burn: Eight Stories for Hanukkah by **Barbara Diamond Goldin.**
Illustrations by Elaine Greenstein.
Viking
ISBN: 0670858757

Each story in this refreshing collection represents a Hanukkah theme, with settings ranging from Biblical times to modern Israel. A few of the stories are original, but most are based on traditional sources.

Hidden Music: The Life of Fanny Mendelssohn by Gloria Kamen.
Atheneum Books for Young Readers
ISBN: 068931714X

Sister of the more famous Felix, Fanny was a dutiful daughter, an adoring sister, and a talented musician in her own right. A well-crafted biography with a restrained but strong feminist thrust.

God's Story: How God Made Mankind by Jan Mark.
Illustrations by David Parkin.
Candlewick Press
ISBN: 0763603767

Following the narrative order of the Tanakh, Mark's retellings are strong, poetic, and subtly witty, capturing the Biblical meaning while sculpting each story into a spare shape that is reflected by the illustrations.

The Garden by Carol Matas.
Simon & Schuster Books for Young Readers
ISBN: 0689803494

Amidst an action-packed plot set in Israel on the eve of independence, this sequel to *After the War* (1996) deals with some of the themes implicit in the founding of the Jewish state.

Passage to Freedom: The Sugihara Story by Ken Mochizuki.
Illustrations by Dom Lee.
Lee and Low
ISBN: 1880000490

Illustrated in sepia tones to resemble old photographs, this recalls a Japanese righteous person through the eyes and voice of a five-year-old boy who witnessed his diplomat father defy official orders and follow his own conscience.

The Koufax Dilemma **by Steven Schnur.**
Illustrations by Meryl Treatner.
Morrow Junior Books
ISBN: 0688142214

Of course Danny will pitch the season's opening game. But what if it's on the first night of Passover?

Of Heroes, Hooks, and Heirlooms **by Faye Silton.**
Jewish Publication Society
ISBN: 082760582X

Told in the first person by a preteen whose parents are Holocaust survivors, this sincere and deeply touching novel about a school project, peer relationships, and family memories will engross adolescent readers.

A Place Not Home **by Eva Wiseman.**
Stoddard Kids
ISBN: 0773758348

Thirteen-year-old Nellie tells the story of her family's harrowing flight from Hungary following the revoluation of 1956, imbuing it with adventure, humor, and humanity as well as hardship.

Teen Readers

Heeding the Call: Jewish Voices in America's Civil Rights Struggle **by Norman H. Finkelstein.**
Jewish Publication Society
ISBN: 0827605909

An even-handed and accurate account of the conflicts and commonalities between American Jews and African-Americans as they have been played out in the arena of civil rights. Includes reference aids.

Sacred Shadows **by Maxine Schur.**
Dials Books
ISBN: 0803722958

The teen-aged heroine struggles with family duty, her own interests, and a foreboding sense that Jews have no place in a Europe succumbing to anti-Semitism and Nazi barbarism. Polished prose and a serious subject.

1996 Awards

Younger Readers

Shalom, Haver: Goodbye, Friend by Barbara Sofer.
Kar-Ben Publishing
ISBN: 0929371976

A photo essay in memory of Yitzhak Rabin, the Israeli prime minister who was assassinated in 1995.

Older Readers

When I Left My Village by Maxine Schur.
Illustrations by Brian Pinkney.
Dial Books
ISBN: 0803715617

An Ethiopian Jewish family leaves their oppressed mountain village to make a difficult and treacherous journey in the hope of reaching freedom in Israel.

Honor Books

Younger Readers

Dybbuk: A Story Made in Heaven by Francine Prose.
Illustrations by Mark Podwal.
Greenwillow Books
ISBN: 0688143075

Because forty days before a baby is born the angels in heaven decide whom it will marry, nothing prevents the wedding of Leah and Chonon from taking place.

Older Readers

Esther's Story by **Diane Wolkstein.**
Illustrations by Juan Wijngaard.
Morrow Junior Books
ISBN: 0688121276

Almost twenty-five centuries ago, a shy orphan girl was unexpectedly chosen as queen of Persia. Blessed with majesty and humanity, she risked the wrath of a king to save her people.

Notable Books

Younger Readers

Becky and Benny Thank God by **Howard Bogot.**
Illustrations by Norman Gorbaty.
CCAR
ISBN: 0881230650

Tiny tots can see, smell and feel creation in this lively, likable board book that mimics the Pat-the-Bunny format. Contents carefully attend to biblical detail; the quality packaging reflects concern for manipulation abilities.

Hirsh's Secret: A Baal Shem Tov Story by **Sterna Citron.**
Illustrations by Igor Eydel.
Kerem
ISBN: 0881230650

A heart-warming tale of the Baal Shem Tov delivers the concept of mitzvoth. A well-developed plot and expressive art solve the mystery of why Hirsh, a *troger* in a Yiddish *shtetl*, is so poor when he has so much goat milk to sell.

Just Stay Put by **Gary Clement.**
Douglas & McIntyre
ISBN: 0888992394

Chelm's illogical logic arrives through outstandingly inventive art that captures the sly humor of the silly plot. Mendel unknowingly retraces his own steps, finds the "new" town just like home, and wonders why he ever left.

Bone Button Borscht by Aubrey Davis.
Illustrations by Dušan Petričić.
Kids Can Press (First US Edition, 1997)
ISBN: 1550742248.

Based on the folktale "Stone Soup," this rollicking, snappy, humorous, ethnic redo serves a Jewish tale of *tzedakah* from the point of view of the beggar. The dialog bursts with Yiddish phrases. Superb art adds to the charm, irony and fun of this delicious book.

The Angel and the Donkey by Katherine Paterson.
Illustrations by Alexander Koshkin.
Clarion Books
ISBN: 0395689694

Dramatic story line, chipper dialogue and rich art combine in this entertaining version of Balaam's talking donkey. The well-paced text stresses God-fearing action and exploits everyone's greedy desires despite their regal positions.

The Jewish Children's Bible: Genesis by Sheryl Prenzlau.
Illustrations by Zely Smelkhov.
Pitspopany Press
ISBN: 0943706319

This upbeat bible retells selected stories from Genesis with major personalities and details in proper Tanach order. Extra lines from *Midrash* suggest motives. The illustrations are not as good as the text.

Older Readers

God's Mailbox: More Stories about Stories in the Bible by Marc Gellman.
Illustrations by Debbie Tilley.
Morrow Junior Books
ISBN: 0688131697

With feeling, humor and bite, Gellman interprets moral lessons in familiar bible stories and unfamiliar one line laws. His point of view is human, his *Midrash* modern. The stories are light hearted, but not light weight.

Celebrating Hanukkah by Diane Hoyt-Goldsmith.
Photographs by Lawrence Migdale.
Holiday House
ISBN: 0823412520

This personal photo essay presents Hanukkah from the joyous point of view of a fifth grade girl. Positive, loving explanations clearly deliver religion, history, tradition, symbols and the significance of all.

***Sky* by Hanneke Ippisch.**
Simon & Schuster Books for Young Readers
ISBN: 068980508X

The memoir is an honest reflection on the author's life, her Holocaust resistanc activities in Holland, imprisonment, and the character of her Dutch compatriots. Poetic language describes pre-war innocence and waer time fear.

Fitting In by Sharon Kirsch.
Second Story Press
ISBN: 0929005740

A peer protagonist shares the tribulations of being different in an age-appropriate initiation into the world where religious identity is baggage. Set in 1960s Canada before ethnic roots were chic, intrinsically Jewish, this delightful read for pre-puberty girls boasts careful plotting, appealing characters, amusing dialogue and genuine emotions.

Four Perfect Pebbles: A HolocaustStory by Lila Perl and Marion Blumenthal Lazan.
Greenwillow Books
ISBN: 068814294X

An innocent hopeful memoir plots the fate of German Jews in Dutch concentration camps. Third person narration recalls a young girl's life metamorphosed from refugee to prisoner to DP to immigrant to positive survivor.

Teddy Kollek: Builder of Jerusalem by Abraham Rabinovich.
Jewish Publication Society
ISBN: 0827605617

Details about the famous mayor of Jerusalem include his days as a Zionist pioneer, gun runner and rescuer of Nazi victims. JPS adds a star to its biography series with this exciting read about a likeable man who liked his life.

The Golem by Barbara Rogasky.
Illustrations by Trina Schart Hyman.
Holiday House
ISBN: 0823409643

Rogasky retells the traditional sci-fi legend of medieval Prague's clay giant in riveting fashion, shrinking not from violence or gore. Sophisticated art frames a strong test for seekers of the dark, dramatic and Gothic.

The Wonder Child and Other Jewish Fairy Tales edited by Howard Schwartz and Barbara Rush.
Illustrations by Stephen Fieser.
HarperCollins
ISBN: 0060235179

The charmed lives of kings and queens, the eerie ones of demons and werewolves involve Jews in this collection of eight fairy tales from various countries. They introduce readers to lore and escapades with Jewish references.

Women of Valor: Stories of Great Jewish Women Who Helped Shape the Twentieth Century by Sheila Segal.
Behrman House
ISBN: 0874416124

Focus on gender, time and mission carries this delightful collection of eight female lives. Each bio is set in a brief world history. The common thread, principle over fame, unites disparate women whose deeds affect us now.

Elie Wiesel: A Voice for Humanity by Ellen Stern.
Jewish Publication Society
ISBN: 0827605749

Evocative words and photographs propel a quiet biography of a famous Holocaust survivor. The author absorbs youngsters in a significant Jewish personality with a dangerous, active youth, but a passive, reflective adulthood.

Back of Beyond: A Bar Mitzvah Journey by Dvora Waysman.
Pitspopany
ISBN: 0943706548

A Jewish boy on a trip to Australia is kidnapped by an Aborigine on his walkabout. Manhood ceremonies drive and solve the plot of this page turner. Jewish identity is a source of personal satisfaction to a realistic teen hero.

Golem by David Wisniewski.
Clarion Books
ISBN: 0395726182

Glorious art (by the author) supports a violent retelling of the legendary Prague Golem. The text turns a medieval thriller into a modern warning against uncontrolled violence. The Caldecott Award winning, multi-layered, three-dimensional paper cuts are fascinating. Illustrations capture light, set an eerie local and propel a giant through mist, flame and smoke.

Unfinished Dreams by Jane Breskin Zalben.
Simon & Schuster Books for Young Readers
ISBN: 0689800339

The "tread carefully" main topics of terminal illness and death are sensitively handled for children. A sixth grade Jewish boy, determined to be a champion violinist, loses his adored elementary school principal and chief supporter to AIDS. Jewish characters are assimilated Americans.

Teen Readers

The Amazing Life of Moe Berg: Catcher, Scholar, Spy by Tricia Andryszewski.
Millbrook Press
ISBN: 1562946102

This well-paced biography presents a genuine eccentric, a famous Jews who was all the subtitle declares. The text, based on letters and clippings, contains many quotes and delivers the brewing World War II as well as the man.

Moe Berg: The Spy behind Home Plate by Vivian Grey.
Jewish Publication Society
ISBN: 0827605862

This is a very detailed biography of an observant Jew who becomes a professional athlete and atomic spy. His wild character stands out despite a worshipful tone. His life will attract non-sports fans to the man and world politics.

Night Flight by Gerald Hausman.
Philomel Books
ISBN: 039922758X

Jewish identity, anti-Semitism, self-awareness and self-worth combine in a plot to discover who poisoned the town dogs. The preteen protagonist sifts moral choices in a scary summer vignette that molds and matures him. A boy's story, the spare autobiographical novel is a dark read for boys and girls.

***Sarah with an H* by Hadley Irwin.**
Margaret K. McElderry Books, an imprint of Simon & Schuster
ISBN: 0689804942

The plot of "new Jewish girl in town triggers prejudice" arrives through female athletes and an unusual point of view. The focus is on anguished reaction to anti-Semitism by the perpetrator, rather than the recipient.

***After the War* by Carol Matas.**
Simon & Schuster
ISBN: 0689803508

This likeable historical novel covers the immediate post war period in short chapters at a fast pace. Fictional characters personalize the drama of Polish Holocaust survivors who escape to Palestine and succeed at illegal entry.

***Gideon's People* by Carolyn Meyer.**
Harcourt Brace
ISBN: 0152003037

Rebellion sparks a compelling story of two preteen boys from immigrant families struggling to keep closed tradition in an alluring open society. A peddler's wagon accident plots groups you wouldn't think of comparing: Orthodox Jews and strict Amish. The theme, "know another to know thy self," moves readers to evaluate friends and heritage.

***Behind the Bedroom Wall* by Laura E. Williams.**
Milkweed Editions
ISBN: 57131606X

A teenager converts from *Bund Deutscher Madel* to Jewish protector after stumbling onto her family's secret -- Jews her parents hide behind her bedroom wall. The decision to report or support them propels a suspenseful plot from the righteous gentile's point of view. The fiction highlights the pivotal importance of parental attitude in creating tolerance.

1995 Awards

Younger Readers

Star of Fear, Star of Hope by Jo Hoestlandt.
Translated by Mark Polizzotti.
Illustrations by Johanna Kang.
Walker and Company
ISBN: 0802775888

Nine-year-old Helen is confused by the disappearance of her Jewish friend during the German occupation of Paris.

Older Readers

Dancing on the Bridge of Avignon by Ida Vos.
Translated by Terese Edelstein and Inez Smidt.
Houghton Mifflin
ISBN: 0395720397

Relates the experiences of a young Jewish girl and her family during the Nazi occupation of the Netherlands.

Honor Books

Younger Readers

The Christmas Menorahs: How a Town Fought Hate by Janice Cohn.
Illustrations by Bill Farnsworth.
Albert Whitman
ISBN: 0807511536

Describes how people in Billings, Montana joined together to fight a series of hate crimes against a Jewish family.

Older Readers

Drummers of Jericho by Carolyn Meyer.
Gulliver Books, an imprint of Harcourt Brace
ISBN: 0152001905

A fourteen-year-old Jewish girl goes to live with her father and stepmother in a small town and soon finds herself the center of a civil rights battle when she objects to the high school band marching in the formation of a cross.

One Yellow Daffodil: A Hanukkah Story by **David Adler.**
Illustrations by Lloyd Bloom.
Gulliver Books, an imprint of Harcourt Brace
ISBN: 0152005374

Two children help a survivor reconnect to his religious tradition when their family includes him in Hanukkah celebrations. He introduces the youngsters to the Holocaust. The art is dark; the text is polite and moving.

Notable Books

Younger Readers

A Yom Kippur Think by **Miriam Feinberg.**
Illustrations by Karen Ostrove.
United Synagogue of Conservative Judaism Commission on Jewish Education

Simple language and engaging pictures state the values of Yom Kippur for Conservative and Reform Jews.

Night Lights: A Sukkot Story by **Barbara Diamond Goldin.**
Illustrations by Louise August.
Gulliver Books, an imprint of Harcourt Brace
ISBN: 0152005366

In a clever slant for a Sukkot story, a little boy overcomes his fear of the dark. He finds security by considering starts as night lights when he sleeps with his sister in the sukkah. The art is refreshing and expressive.

When a Grandparent Dies by **Nechama Liss-Levinson.**
Jewish Lights Publishing
ISBN: 1879045443

Part journal, part lesson, all heart, this sensitive, useful book guides a youngster through *shiva* and the year after, supporting memory, grief and other feelings.

When Solomon Was King by Sheila MacGill-Callahan.
Illustrations by Stephen Johnson.
Dial Books for Younger Readers
ISBN: 0803715897

Solomon's ability to speak to animals underlies an apocryphal basis of why Jews don't hunt.

The Matzah That Papa Brought Home by Fran Manushkin.
Illustrations by Ned Bittinger.
Scholastic Books
ISBN: 0590471465

A cumulative "House That Jack Built"-type rhyme captures the traditions and history of the Seder. Family and Passover bask in humor and fond memory through text and misty art.

Starlight and Candles by Fran Manushkin.
Illustrations by Jacqueline Chwast.
Simon & Schuster Books for Young Readers
ISBN: 0689802749

Delightful art delivers a warm story about three generations of a modern family as they prepare for and celebrate Shabbat at home and in the synagogue.

Strudel, Strudel, Strudel by Steve Sanfield.
Illustrations by Emily Lisker.
Orchard Books
ISBN: 053106879X

Superb, stylized art delivers Sanfield's version of the Chelm story about the couple who roll down the hill in a trunk. The text is upbeat, fun, silliness laced with logic and human frailty.

The Tie Man's Miracle: A Chanukkah Tale by Steven Schnur.
Illustrations by Stephen Johnson.
Morrow Junior Books
ISBN: 0688134627

A young boy hears about the Holocaust for the first time from a salesman who joins the family Chanukkah. The old man recounts the power of the last night's candles; the boy makes a poignant wish for him. The art is realistic.

Passover Magic by **Roni Schotter.**
Illustrations by Marilyn Hafner.
Little Brown
ISBN: 0316774685

Passover brings an energetic family together; even though the magician uncle is outdone by the wonders of Seder preparation in observance. Words and art reflect warmth, humor and happy Judaism at a manic pace.

The Golden City: Jerusalem's 3000 Years by **Neil Waldman.**
Atheneum Books for Young Readers
ISBN: 0689800800
This chronological reflection on Jerusalem's history sets a text focusing on competitors for the city in glorious art (by the author) which captures landmarks in glowing light.

Older Readers

Child of the Warsaw Ghetto by **David Adler.**
Illustrations by Karen Ritz.
Holiday House
ISBN: 0823411605

This slim, grim volume chronologically details the Ghetto's graphic history through a surviving child.

Listen to the Trees by **Molly Cone.**
Illustrations by Roy Doty.
UAHC
ISBN: 0807405361

A Tu B'Shvat resource tool recounts the ancient and continuing nexus between Judaism and ecology. Stories, cartoons and quotes of uneven quality mix in a well-organized format.

Ezra Jack Keats: A Biography with Illustrations by **Dean Engel and Florence Freedman.**
Silver Moon Press
ISBN: 1881889653

Surprise! A beloved children's author-illustrator is Jewish, not black, as everyone deduces from his famous pictures. His life provides a lesson on anti-Semitism in secular careers; he hid his Judaism to succeed, not survive.

How Do You Spell God?: Answers to the Big Questions from Around the World by Marc Gellman and Thomas Hartman.
Illustrations by Joseph A. Smith.
Morrow Junior Books
ISBN: 0688130410

A thoughtful, clever volume explains major world religions according to the meaningful questions they answer, and compares them through their different answers. The authors sport "with it" voice and humorous drawings.

Bat Mitzvah by Barbara Diamond Goldin.
Illustrations by Erika Weihs.
Viking
ISBN: 0670860344

Bat Mitzvah from the point of view of an outsider who wants to understand. The focus is history and changing ancient tradition in our century, in our country. The tone is feminist/didactic. Illustrations are charming.

The Adventures of Hershel of Ostropol by Eric A. Kimmel.
Illustrations by Trina Schart Hyman.
Holiday House
ISBN: 08234322105

Ten classic stories about poor, but clever Hershel of Ostropol abound in humorous Yiddish culture. A separate chapter quotes his witty epigrams.

Bar Mitzvah by Eric A. Kimmel.
Illustrations by Erika Weihs.
Viking
ISBN: 0670855405

Bar Mitzvah from the point of view of the participant who performs as expected and wishes he knew more. The focus is memory and meaning. The tone is warm and sharing. The illustrations are charming.

Ordinary Genius: The Story of Albert Einstein by Stephanie McPherson.
Carolrhoda Books
ISBN: 0876147880

Clear prose and great photographs advance a chronological narration of Einstein's life, theories of space and time, eccentric habits and fame. He is proud of his Jewish identity and connects its teachings to his acts.

Isaac Bashevis Singer: The Life of a Storyteller by Lila Perl.
Illustrations by Donna Ruff.
Jewish Publication Society
ISBN: 0827605129

This laudatory life of Singer gains charm from facts about his Polish youth and full-page sketches.

Golem: A Giant Made of Mud by Mark Podwal.
Greenwillow Books
ISBN: 068813811X

Imaginative, historically detailed paintings by the author adorn this remarkable retelling of the classic Golem in Prague folklore including Rabbi Loew and the emperor's fascination with alchemy. Lovely art is striking in a scary story.

Bearing Witness: Stories of the Holocaust edited by Hazel Rochman and Darlene Z McCampbell.
Orchard Books
ISBN: 053109488X

Carefully selected, brilliantly pared and well-arranged literary excerpts from long works create a comprehensive chronological Holocaust history which builds in tension, interest and emotion. Superb for classroom use.

The Rose Horse by Deborah Lee Rose.
Illustrations by Greg Shed.
Harcourt Brace
ISBN: 0152000682

The information is fresh: Yiddish immigrants carving carousel horses, Coney Island side show incubators saving premature babies, the counting of the Omer. Local color is turn of the century. Pencil sketches fit the tone.

Flying Lessons by Nava Semel.
Translated by Hillel Halkin.
Simon & Schuster Books for Young Readers
ISBN: 0689801610

A bittersweet story romanticizes the time when Israel was a new state through a humorous teen narrator stuck in a provincial town. A sensitive shoemaker teaches her to balance dreams and reality through his Holocaust experience which is portrayed in original symbols.

Yoni Netanyahu: Commando at Entebbe by **Devra Speregen.**
Jewish Publication Society
ISBN: 0827605234

An Israeli hero is a role model in this reprise of the stirring 1976 raid on Entebbe he led.

Life in the Warsaw Ghetto by **Gail B. Stewart.**
Lucent Books
ISBN: 1560060751

All the ugly details of the Warsaw Ghetto and the Jews who suffered there are documented in this emotionally tough book. The photographs are incredible. The lesson is clear: it never should have happened.

Legends of the Chinese Jews of Kaifeng by **Xin Xu with Beverly Friend.**
Illustrations by Ting Cheng.
KTAV
ISBN: 0881255289

Oral legends chronologically detail the curious history of 1000 years of Judaism in Kaifeng, China.

And Twelve Chinese Acrobats by **Jane Yolen.**
Illustrations by Jean Gralley.
Philomel Books
ISBN: 0399226915

Spirited language and pictures mesh in this brisk biographical tale of the idolized, mischievous older brother sent away to military school. It is rich in humor and Russian-Jewish rituals and tradition.

Teen Readers

Under the Domim Tree by **Gila Almagor.**
Translated by Hillel Schenker.
Simon & Schuster Books for Young Readers
ISBN: 0671890204

Three teens in an Israeli youth village after the Holocaust deal with tough emotions sharpened by German war reparations in Israel. They search for lost parents and confront survivor guilt in this autobiographical novel.

Parallel Journeys by Eleanor H. Ayer, Helen Waterford and Alfons Heck.
Atheneum Books for Young Readers
ISBN: 0689318308

Holocaust experiences from both sides simultaneously! A Jewish girl and a Naziboy alternate voice revealing what happened, confessing how it felt, and deducing moral lessons.

Broken Bridge by Lynne Reid Banks.
Morrow Junior Books
ISBN: 0688135951

A sensitive look at the Israel-Palestinian Arab conflict opens with the murder of an American teen in Israel. In this sequel (25 years later) to *One More River*, the extended family faces the consequences along with relevant politics, minimum violence and romance.

Look to the Hills by Hazel Krantz.
Jewish Publication Society
ISBN: 0827605528

Local color fills this romance set in late 19th century Colorado which details a thriving Reform Jewish community and the origin of the Jewish Hospital. A chart explains real and imagined characters.

But Can the Phoenix Sing? by Christa Laird
Greenwillow Books
ISBN: 0688136125

An angry teen discovers the incredible details of his stern stepfather's partisan career during World War II in a wide-ranging story that contains heroic information scantily covered in YA fiction.

Days of Judgment: The World War II War Crimes Trials by Isobel V. Morin.
Millbrook
ISBN: 1562944428

This is a clear, concise evaluation of the Nuremberg and Tokyo trials. Photographs and no-frills vocabulary combine to weigh facts, sift results, recall prevailing passions and establish contemporary relevance.

Fat Chance by Lesléa Newman.
G.P. Putnam's
ISBN: 0399227601

Through diary entries, a teen recounts her struggles to lose weight, hide her bulimia from her mother, find a boyfriend and a career. It's a mainstream novel with a comfortably Jewish heroine, humorous and moving.

The Lady with the Hat by Uri Orlev.
Translatedby Hillel Halkin.
Houghton Mifflin
ISBN: 0395699576

A teen survivor in Poland joins a group of young people headed for a Palestine kibbutz unaware that his sole living relative, now an English citizen, is looking for him. Readers follow an exciting man hunt.

1994 Awards

Younger Readers

The Always Prayer Shawl by Sheldon Oberman.
Illustrations by Ted Lewin.
Boyds Mill Press
ISBN: 0140561579

A prayer shawl is handed down from grandfather to grandson in this story of Jewish tradition and the passage of generations.

Older Readers

The Shadow Children by Steven Schnur.
Illustrations by Herbert Tauss.
Morrow Junior Books
ISBN: 0688138314

While spending the summer on his grandfather's farm in the French countryside, eleven-year-old Etienne discovers a secret dating back to World War II and encounters the ghosts of Jewish children who suffered a dreadful fate under the Nazis.

Honor Books
Younger Readers

Day of Delight: A Jewish Sabbath in Ethiopia by Maxine Schur.
Illustrations by Brian Pinkney.
Dial Books for Young Readers
ISBN: 0803714149

Depicts a young Ethiopian Jewish boy and his family, including their typical daily routine followed by preparation for and celebration of the Sabbath.

Older Readers

One Foot Ashore by Jacqueline Dembar Greene.
Walker and Company
ISBN: 0802776019

Arriving alone and destitute in Amsterdam in the spring of 1654, sixteen-year-old Maria Ben Lazar finds refuge and friendship in the household of the artist Rembrandt and continues to search for her parents and her younger sister.

Notable Books
Younger Readers

Northern Lights: A Hanukkah Story by Diana Conway.
Illustrations by Shelly O. Haas.
Kar-Ben Publishing
ISBN: 0929371798

Sara is grounded in a remote Eskimo village by a storm. She shares an unusual Hanukkah celebration interwoven with Eskimo customs.

After the Flood by Arthur Geisert.
Houghton Mifflin
ISBN: 039566612

Imaginative and visually appealing to the youngest child, this is a hopeful account of Noah's family life after the ark was left on Mount Ararat.

Don't Forget by Patricia Lakin.
Illustrations by Ted Rand.
Tambourine Books
ISBN: 0688120768

Little Sarah, wanting to bake a surprise birthday cake for her mother, learns that one must remember "bad things" so they won't happen again. The book can be shared with a child who may be too young to ask about the Holocaust.

Tikvah Means Hope by Patricia Polacco.
Delacorte Press, an imprint of Random House
ISBN: 0385320590

With focus on the environment and concern for living creatures, this colorful, pastel-crayoned story interweaves Succot and Thanksgiving. Placed during the terrible Oakland fire, the cat named Tikvah symbolizes a rebirth and rebuilding of the community.

Matzah Ball by Mindy Avra Portnoy.
Illustrations by Katherine Janus Kahn.
Kar-Ben Publishing
ISBN: 0929371682

An original Passover story, especially for boys, based on the Elijah legend. The book has an entertaining baseball theme with a moral about Jewish dietary restrictions. It will appeal to second and third graders.

King Solomon and the Bee adapted by Dalia Hardof Renberg.
Illustrations by Ruth Heller.
HarperCollins Publishers
ISBN: 0060229020

This is an adaptation of a traditional Jewish legend written decades ago by Hayyim Nahman Bialik. It is the story of a small bee who repays King Solomon for his mercy, presented with finely detailed, gloriously colorful illustrations suitable for story hour.

Older Readers

The Night Crossing by **Karen Ackerman.**
Illustrations by Elizabeth Sayles.
Alfred A. Knopf, an imprint of Random House
ISBN: 067983169X

Mama's Sabbath candlesticks become the focal point of the suspenseful 1938 escape from Austria. Written for second and third graders, with large print and wonderful black and white pencil drawings, it is an excellent introduction to the events of the Holocaust.

Hilde and Eli: Children of the Holocaust by **David A. Adler.**
Illustrations by Karen Ritz.
Holiday House
ISBN: 3823410919

A moving introduction to the Holocaust through an account of the short lives of two young victims. Hilde's life in Frankfurt and Eli's in rural Czechoslovakia under the Nazi onslaught are depicted through straightforward text and subtly toned illustrations.

Tell Them We Remember: The Story of the Holocaust by **Susan D. Bachrach.**
Little Brown and Company
ISBN: 031669264

A photo and textbook of many individual lives drawn from the United States Holocaust Memorial Museum in Washington, DC. Collection of artifacts, photos, maps, and histories. The book presents powerfully documented stories of people who did and did not survive. Complete with bibliography, glossary and index

The Old Brown Suitcase by **Lillian Boraks-Nemetz.**
BenSimon Publications
ISBN: 0914539108

Documentary fiction written by a Polish Holocaust survivor who made it to Canada with her parents in 1947. The story works on the problems of adjustment and resettlement for a teenaged girl who must deal with her trauma of the war years.

Make a Wish Molly by Barbara Cohen.
Illustrations by Jan Naimo Jones.
Doubleday Books for Young Readers
ISBN: 038531079X

A Passover sequel to *Molly's Pilgrim* (published posthumously) this story is about the alienation of a Jewish child in a strange, new land, compounded by the restrictions of Jewish dietary laws. This elementary school level story highlights realistic childhood experiences and feelings and will be excellent for classroom discussion.

Myriam Mendilow, Mother of Jerusalem by Barry and Phyllis Cytron.
Lerner Publications
ISBN: 0822549190

The life of Myriam Mendilow is a monument to the values of persistent hard work and creative imagination. Written for grades five and up, it is about the founder of Jerusalem's Lifeline for the Old projects, a modern day Jewish heroine.

The Family Treasury of Jewish Holidays by Malka Drucker.
Illustrations by Nancy Patz.
Little Brown and Company
ISBN: 0316193437

This is a beautifully presented collection of favorite, previously published stories, poems and songs assembled to help parents and teachers share ideas and values crucial to each Jewish holiday, with children of all ages. The book includes chapters of Tu B'Shvat, Yom HaShoah and Yom HaAtzma'ut.

The Passover Journey: A Seder Companion by Barbara Diamond Goldin.
Illustrations by Neil Waldman.
Pengion Group
ISBN: 0670824216

Explained as an annual journey, the Seder, both ancient and current, is made meaningful for children in the third grade and older. The art work is exquisite, creating a treasured volume of information.

Grey Striped Shirt: How Grandma and Grandpa Survived the Holocaust by
Jacqueline Jules.
Illustrations by Michael Cressy.
Alef Design Group
ISBN: 1881283062

A large print, comparatively gentle Holocaust story, told for third and fourth
graders, brings out the thoughts and feelings of survivors. It underlines the message
"we will not forget."

Escape from Egypt by Sonia Levitin.
Little Brown and Company
ISBN: 0316522732

An exciting, imaginative retelling of the Exodus expanded and embroidered with
drama, love and serious discussion of religious belief. It is well written with finely
developed fictional as well as historical characters, suitable both for young and
more mature adults.

1993 Awards

Younger Readers

The Uninvited Guest by Nina Jaffe.
Illustrations by Elivia Savadier.
Scholastic
ISBN: 0590446533

Includes background information and retellings of traditional tales from Jewish
folklore and legend related to major holidays, such as Yom Kippur, Sukkot,
Hanukkah, and Purim.

Older Readers

Sworn Enemies by Carol Matas.
Bantam Doubleday Dell
ISBN: 0533083260

In nineteenth-century Russia, betrayed by a fellow Jew, sixteen-year-old Aaron is
taken by officers of the Czar and forced into military service.

Honor Books

Younger Readers

Neve Shalom Wahat Al-Salam: Oasis of Peace by Laurie Dolphin.
Photographss by Ben Dolphin.
Scholastic
ISBN: 0590457993

Text and photos present the lives of two boys, one Jewish and one Arab, who attend school in a unique community near Jerusalem where Jews and Arabs live together in peace.

A Candle for Grandpa by David Techner and Judith Techner.
Illustrations by Joel Iskowitz.
UAHC Press
ISBN: 0807405078

A young boy describes the events surrounding the death of his grandfather including his and his family's feelings of grief and the Jewish funeral service that they participate in. Also includes answers to frequently asked questions regarding death and funerals.

Older Readers

Raoul Wallenberg: The Man Who Stopped Death by Sharon Linnea.
Jewish Publication Society
ISBN: 0827604483

Traces the life of the Swedish diplomat who saved Hungarian Jews during World War II and then mysteriously disappeared after the Russians occupied Budapest.

Notable Books

Younger Readers

The Kingdom of the Singing Birds by Miriam Aroner.
Illustrations by Shelly O. Haas.
Kar-Ben Publishing
ISBN: 0929371437

A beautifully illustrated story of Rabbi Zusya, wise in the ways of nature, and of a young king who did not understand that birds must be free in order to sing. A Hasidic tale teaching honesty and courage.

***The Gift* by Aliana Brodmann.**
Illustrations by Anthony Carnabuci.
Simon & Schuster Books for Young Readers
ISBN: 0671751107

Through tender, muted illustrations and carefully chosen descriptive text, the joy of giving *tzedakah* is beautifully taught for first through third grades.

***Blessed Are You* by Michelle Edwards.**
Lothrop, Lee & Shepard
ISBN: 068810759

A collection of colorfully illustrated Jewish blessings that express joy, grief, and praise.

***David and Goliath* by Leonard Everett Fisher.**
Holiday House
ISBN: 082340997

Well-detailed, sensitively handled text of this dramatic confrontation. Suitable for both Jewish and non-Jewish children of a very young age.

***The Magician's Visit* by Barbara Diamond Goldin.**
Illustrations by Robert Andrew Parker.
Viking
ISBN: 067084840

An artistic version of a well-known Peretz tale. Simple text harmoniously united with Chagall-like illustrations about Elijah's visit to a poor *shtetl* couple at Passover.

***God Must Like Cookies, Too* by Carol Snyder.**
Illustrations by Beth Glick.
Jewish Publication Society
ISBN: 08277604238

A little girl spends an entire Friday with her grandmother. It is a sweet account of a Reform Sabbath service for very young children.

Pot Luck by Tobi Tobias.
Illustrations by Nola Langer Malone.
Lothrop, Lee & Shepard
ISBN: 0152208704

Grandmother spends a day with granddaughter Rachel, preparing a "pot luck" dinner for a life-long friend from Poland. The flashback illustrations and those of shopping, cleaning, baking and cooking are a large part of the pleasure in this book.

Light: The First Seven Days by Sarah Waldman.
Illustrations by Neil Waldman.
Harcourt Brace Jovanovich
ISBN: 0152208704

The six days of Creation unfold in simple, well-chosen words and a mosaic of colorful paintings. It is an excellent book for sharing in front of a group of small children.

Hanukkah, Oh Hanukkah compiled by Wendy Wax.
Illustrations by John Speirs.
Bantam Books
ISBN: 053309551X

A scrapbook of how-to information covering holiday history, food, games, prayers, stories, songs, poetry, and four wonderful memoirs geared for the modern family.

Stone Men by Nicki Weiss.
Greenwillow Books
ISBN: 0688110169

A tale of a mute Jewish peddler who finds a unique way to save a *shtetl* from attack. The story has fine, descriptive vocabulary suitable for storytelling.

Older Readers

Jacob's Rescue by Malka Drucker and Michael Halperin.
Doubleday
ISBN: 05330897605

Based on a real-life situation, it is a story about the Jews and their Polish protectors during the Holocaust. Proper honor is paid to the Righteous Gentiles in this story.

The Golem and the Dragon Girl by **Sonia Levitin.**
Dial Books
ISBN: 0806712812

A teenage daughter of Chinese immigrants meets Jonathan, a Jewish teenager living with his mom and a new stepfather. Two cultures come together comfortably in a series of ghostly happenings: a serious accident and a reconciliation of dilemmas. A book for fun and acquiring unusual information for teenage boys and girls.

Sweet Notes, Sour Notes by **Nancy Smiler Levinson.**
Lodestar, an imprint of Dutton
ISBN: 0525673792

David's close relationship with his *Zayde* and their shared love of music provide a nostalgic look at life in the 1920's. Positive values are given without preaching.

Lydia, Queen of Palestine by **Uri Orlev.**
Translated by Hillel Haklin.
Houghton Mifflin
ISBN: 0395656605

Lydia is bright, talented and exasperating. This is her adventure from Romania to life on an Israeli kibbutz. It is fast-paced and humorous for readers ten to fourteen.

Tell Me a Mitzvah by **Danny Siegel.**
Kar-Ben Publishing
ISBN: 092937178X

A collection of inspiring vignettes about performing mitzvoth. Included is a "What Can I Do?" series, consisting of pages of ideas so that parents and children can make a difference.

Behind the Secret Window by **Nelly S. Toll.**
Dial Books
ISBN: 0803713622

A personal Holocaust account told in breathless chronology from 1941 through 1944. The story is enriched by remarkable watercolor art work done behind the secret window. This is a fine companion piece to *The Diary of Anne Frank.*

Anne Frank: Beyond the Diary by **Ruud van der Rol and Rian Verhoeven.**
Translated by Tony Langham and Plym Peters.
Viking Children's Books
ISBN: 0670849324

This photo-biography presents Anne's life through the family's photo album, in addition to selections from the famous diary. This book can serve well as supplementary text for a beginning Holocaust study.

Anna is Still Here by Ida Vos.
Translated by Terese Edelstein and Inez Smidt.
Houghton Mifflin
ISBN: 0395653681

Set in northern Holland, this is a deeply disturbing account of a traumatized 13-year-old girl. The deep meaning of the Sabbath celebration and Anna's love of books offset the uncomfortable feelings young teens may experience when reading this compelling story.

The Warsaw Ghetto Uprising by Karen Zeinert.
Millbrook Press
ISBN: 1562942824

This is an excellent basic text for the study of Jewish resistance during World War II. Written in simple language, it is so carefully researched that it is suitable for upper high school grades and college level.

1992 Awards

Younger Readers

Something from Nothing by Phoebe Gilman.
North Winds Press, an imprint of Scholastic Canada
ISBN: 059073802X

In this retelling of a traditional Jewish folktale, Joseph's baby blanket is transformed into ever smaller items as he grows until there is nothing left--but then Joseph has an idea.

Older Readers

Letters from Rifka by Karen Hesse.
Henry Holt
ISBN: 0140363912

In letters to her cousin, a young Jewish girl chronicles her family's flight from Russia in 1919 and her own experiences when she must be left in Belgium for a while when the others immigrate to America.

Honor Books

Younger Readers

Jeremy's Dreidel by Ellie Gellman.
Illustrations by Judith Friedman.
Kar-Ben Publishing
ISBN: 092937133X

Jeremy signs up for a Hanukkah workshop to make unusual dreidels and creates a clay dreidel with braille dots for his dad, who is blind.

Riches by Esther Hautzig.
Illustrations by Donna Diamond.
Harper Collins
ISBN: 006022259

This finalist for the 1993 Jewish Book Award tells of an old man and woman in a little Eastern European village who are given some surprising advice from a wise rabbi. They have worked hard, raised a family, and given generously to the poor, but they come to realize what is missing from their lives--and where their riches really lie. – Ingram, www.amazon.com

The Spotted Pony: A Collection of Hanukkah Stories by Eric A. Kimmel.
Illustrations by Leonard Everett Fisher.
Holiday House
ISBN: 0823409368

Eight traditional *shammes* stories--about King Solomon and his magic ring, a mysterious spotted pony, Benayahu ben Yehoyada, and other heroes, demons, and fools--help celebrate the Festival of Lights.

Journey to the Golden Land by Richard Rosenblum.
Jewish Publication Society
ISBN: 082760405X

Having left oppressive czarist Russia in search of better living conditions, Benjamin and his family endure the difficult journey and land at Ellis Island to start a new life in America.

The Sabbath Lion: A Jewish Folktale from Algeria by Howard Schwartz and
Barbara Rush.
Illustrations by Stephen Fieser.
Harper Collins
ISBN: 0060208538

Because of Yosef's devotion to honoring the Sabbath, he is given special protection
by a great lion during a dangerous journey through the desert.

Older Readers

Tunes for Bears to Dance to **by Robert Cormier.**
Delacorte Press, an imprint of Random House
ISBN: 0440219035

Eleven-year-old Henry escapes his family's problems by watching the woodcarving
of Mr. Levine, an elderly Holocaust survivor, but when Henry is manipulated into
betraying his friend he comes to know true evil.

Notable Books

Younger Readers

David's Songs: His Psalms and Their Story **by Colin T. Eisler.**
Illustrations by Jerry Pinkney.
Dial Books
ISBN: 0803710585

In a most beautifully illustrated book, the author has presented to young readers a
selection of Psalms so well-chosen and so skillfully arranged and translated, that
they will be read and enjoyed by youngsters of all faiths who have an interest in
history, poetry, and art.

In the Month of Kislev: A Story of Hanukkah **by Nina Jaffe.**
Illustrations by Louise August.
Viking
ISBN: 0670828637

This is a very beautifully illustrated Hanukkah tale in which a wealthy and nasty
head of a family learn an important lesson. The result is that he welcomes a poor
family into the midst of his own family so that they all can celebrate together.

Through this lovely story, children will learn Hanukkah customs as well as the mitzvah of sharing with the poor.

Mrs. Katz and Tush by Patricia Polacco.
Bantam
ISBN: 0553081225

In Ms. Polacco's tradition of excellence, this is a very beautifully illustrated and sensitively written book about an old Jewish widow's growing friendship with her African American neighbor's son, Larnel. The closeness is woven through another "friend," an uninvited kitten adopted by Mrs. Katz, who named it *tush* (Yiddish for bottom) because the cat doesn't have a tail.

Elijah's Angel: A Story for Chanukah and Christmas by Michael J. Rosen.
Illustrations by Aminah Brenda Lynn Robinson.
Harcourt Brace Jovanovich
ISBN: 0152253947

Elijah is a barber and woodcarver. Michael, a young Jewish boy, is befriended by him. Michael admires Elijah for his wonderful creativity, but he is well aware of the important differences between their faiths, and does not know whether his parents will accept this friendship. Hopefully the book will become an example of how we can live together, learn from one another, and yet remain proud and knowledgeable of our differences.

Joshua's Dream by Sheila Segal.
Illustrations by Joel Iskowitz.
UAHC
ISBN: 0807404764

What a refreshing little book! Just when we were told that Zionism was dead, UAHC re-issues and updates a beautiful book for young children about the essence of Zionism -- love for the land of Israel. Little Joshua learns about a family member who was a pioneer when he arrives for this first to Israel. Just as he plants a seedling in the desert, so his love for the land is gently sown to grow and flourish to maturity.

Older Readers

Children of Bach **by Eilis Dillon.**
Macmillan
ISBN: 0684194406

This is a sensitively written book about the escape of one part of a Hungarian family from the onslaught of the Nazis toward the end of World War II. Cowardice, bravery and all the feelings in between surface as the group of six escapees live in very close quarters. Though this group never totally lost its human dignity, many situations occurred in which they were tested to the extreme.

The Store That Mama Built **by Robert Lehrman.**
Macmillan
ISBN: 0027546322

A lovely book that tells the story of a large immigrant family's adjustment to life in America, the move from New York City to a small Pennsylvania town, the loss of a father and the struggle of the mother of six to keep a grocery store going and thus make a living for her brood. There are many Yiddish words and expressions used throughout the book. Attempts are made to include Jewish traditions and to explain Jewish customs. Some of the social problems of the era are exposed.

Ellis Island: Land of Hope **by Joan Lowery Nixon.**
Bantam Books
ISBN: 0553081101

This is one of several books written recently on the subject of Jewish immigration from Eastern Europe to the United States. Many feelings are explored in these books: the pains of separation from loved ones and from the familiar; the fear of the new; and the difficult trip by land and sea and then the possibility of not being allowed into the United States through Ellis Island.

The Holocaust: The World and the Jews, 1933-1945 **by Seymour Rossel.**
Behrman House
ISBN: 0874415292

A very well done text for teaching the Holocaust. The use of photographs, official documents, memoirs, diaries and journals, and the clear arrangement of these materials is superb. Teachers and students alike will benefit greatly from this book.

Shalom, Geneva Peace **by Phyllis Shalant.**
Dutton
ISBN: 0525448683

A story about the pains and difficulties of growing up: loneliness, the need for friendships, peer pressure, alienation from parents, the search for attention, and mainly about learning to care, to love and to understand. Andi and Geneva, both 15 years old, change in the course of the novel. The author is certainly in touch with adolescent feelings and behavior.

1991 Awards

Younger Readers

Cakes and Miracles: A Purim Tale by Barbara Diamond Goldin.
Illustrations by Erika Weihs.
Viking
ISBN: 067083047X

Young, blind Hershel finds that he has special gifts he can use to help his mother during the Jewish holiday of Purim.

Daddy's Chair by Sandy Lanton.
Illustrations by Shelly O. Haas.
Kar-Ben Publishing
ISBN: 0929371526

When Michael's father dies his family sits shiva, observing the Jewish week of mourning, and remembers the good things about him.

Older Readers

The Diamond Tree: Jewish Tales from Around the World by Howard Schwartz and Barbara Rush.
Illustrations by Uri Shulevitz.
Harper CollinsISBN: 0064406954

A collection of Jewish traditional nursery tales from many different countries.

Notable Books

Younger Readers

Around the Table: Family Stories of Sholom Aleichem by Sholem Aleichem.
Selected and translated by Aliza Shevrin.
Illustrations by Toby Gowing.
Charles Scribner & Sons
ISBN: 0684192373

These familiar stories, recalling a long-gone era and describing holidays in the bosom of families in an Eastern European *shtetl*, are masterpieces of charms and wisdom, as well as a faithful mirror of Jewish life, tradition and values. The translator managed to convey the flavor of Jewish life and preserve many of the Yiddish idioms; it hardly seems a translation at all.

A Baker's Portrait by **Michelle Edwards.**
Lothrop, Lee & Shepard
ISBN: 068809712X

The same funny, colorful illustrations that delighted readers in *Chicken Man* now create a story that entertains on several different levels. Michelin is an artist who is compelled to draw only what she sees and finds herself in the uncomfortable position of having to reconcile her honesty with the reality of her subjects. Even young children unfamiliar with the concept of metaphors can appreciate Michelin's brilliant solution.

Just Enough Room by **Miriam Feinberg.**
Illustrations by Marlene L. Ruthen.
United   Synagogue of America, Commission on Jewish Education
ISBN: 0838107354

In this lovely story for young children, the tiny, dark house of an older couple expands and grows cheerful on Shabbat as more and more guests arrive for dinner. There is always "just enough room." The magic of Shabbat and the joy of hospitality is attractively demonstrated and aided by Ms. Ruthen's graphic illustrations.

All the Lights of the Night by **Arthur A. Levine.**
Illustrations by James Ransome.
Tambourine Press
ISBN: 0688101070

A charming addition to the extensive picture book literature on Hanukkah. It is the tale of two boys who travel from Russiato Palestine with tickets sent by their older brother. The family's Hanukkah lamp becomes their own private miracle lamp.

Appleblossom by Shulamith Levey Oppenheim.
Illustrations by Joanna Yardley.
Harcourt, Brace, Javonovich
ISBN: 0152037500

A delightful new Passover story about a talking cat who is well versed in Jewish customs and traditions. Appleblossom utilizes her extensive knowledge of Jewish holiday lore to serve her "cat-ty" needs, and those of the little boy who loves her. The large-size, gentle and colorful illustrations suit the subject and age level well.

Toby Belfer Never Had a Christmas Tree by Gloria Teles Pushker.
Illustrations by Judith Hierstein.
Pelican
ISBN: 0882898558

A charming memoir by a little Louisiana girl who joined her friends at their homes to celebrate Christmas; at Hanukkah they joined her to light the candles, eat latkes, play dreidel, and hear the story of Hanukkah. This sharing prevented Toby from feeling that she was being denied an attractive celebration. The language is simple and the illustrations particularly lovely.

Buba Leah and Her Paper Children by Lillian Hammer Ross.
Illustrations by Mary Morgan.
Jewish Publication Society
ISBN: 0827603754

The author manages to sensitively portray the isolation of the immigrant family. This separation from the colorful yet difficult life of the shtetl left a void in their lives, and in the lives of those left behind as well. The story explores the balance achieved between successful settlement in the New World and the cost of this new-found happiness.

Let the Celebrations Begin! by Margaret Wild.
Illustrations by Julie Vivas.
Orchard
ISBN: 0531059375

This moving book tells the story of making toys for child survivors of the Belsen concentration camp. The illustrations realistically depict the conditions of the inmates while preserving their humanity. The accompanying text allows the book to be enjoyed by an older age group than the picture book format might suggest.

Older Readers

Marc Chagall, Painter of Dreams **by Natalie S. Bober.**
Illustrations by Vera Rosenberry.
Jewish Publication Society
ISBN: 0827603797

The painter Marc Chagall is transformed into the man Marc Chagall in this skillfully executed "JPS Young Biography." The warm family life he experienced while growing up and his warm relationship with this first wife, Bella, help the reader to understand the themes of many of his works. The tale of his odyssey from Vitebsk to New York is an especially intriguing section of the book. Rosenberry's illustrations complement the text well.

The Atonement of Mindy Wise **by Marilyn Kaye.**
Harcourt Brace Jovanovich
SBN: 0152004025

Yom Kippur services let Mindy reflect on the sins she has committed during her thirteenth year, when she was desperately anxious to get into a popular crowd at her new middle school.

Waiting for Anya **by Michael Marpugo.**
Viking
ISBN: 0670837350

This is a realistic World War II novel set in Vichy, France at the time of the German occupation. A teenaged boy, Jo, participates in a courageous plan to save Jewish children despite the obvious danger. The suspense and human drama -- a father hopes to find his daughter in each new group of rescued children -- provides exciting and interesting reading.

The Man from the Other Side **by Uri Orlev.**
Translated by Hillel Halkin.
Houghton Mifflin
ISBN: 0395538084

Another fine work on the Shoah, this book tells of a Polish boy who lived in Warsaw during the Warsaw Ghetto Uprising. The realistic presentation of his experiences will give readers insight into the many underlying facets of life under both normal and trying circumstances. (Mildred L. Batchelder Award for Most Outstanding Children's Book in Translation, 1992)

***The Feather Merchants and Other Tales of the Fools of Chelm* by Steve Sanfield.**
Illustrations by Mikhail Magaril.
Orchard Books
ISBN: 0531059588

This version of the well-known Chelm stories is rich with "*tam*" and punctuated with the customs of the Jews of Central Europe. This is not just a book of humorous tales, but is a valuable resource for librarians and teachers; the afterword alone is a notable treasure. Sanfield states, "a simple research trip became a journey of the soul...", and indeed his text accomplishes the same.

***Hide and Seek* by Ida Vos.**
Translated by Terese Edelstein and Inez Smidt.
Houghton Mifflin
ISBN: 0395564700

Based on the author's life as a child, this documentary fiction takes place during the German occupation of Holland during World War II. Through a child's eyes we experience the terror of the German invasion of the Netherlands, the sadness of relinquishing a favorite bicycle, and the constant fear of discovery while hiding in the home of Christian friends. The book is the author's tribute to those courageous friends who helped her and other survive.

***The Fortuneteller in 5B* by Jane Breskin Zalben.**
Henry Holt
ISBN: 080501537X

11-year-old Alexandria Pilaf is grieving over the recent death of her father when a mysterious new neighbor arrives. While pursuing the mystery, she experiences a painful revelation that leads to personal growth and an acceptance of her unique neighbor.

1990 Awards

Younger Readers

The Chanukkah Guest by Eric Kimmel.
Illustrations by Giora Carmi.
Holiday House
ISBN: 0823409783

On the first night of Chanukkah, Old Bear wanders into Bubba Brayna's house and receives a delicious helping of potato *latkes* when she mistakes him for the rabbi.

Older Readers

My Grandmother's Stories by Adèle Geras.
Illustrations by Jael Jordan.
Alfred A. Knopf
ISBN: 0679809104

As a young girl spends time at her grandmother's apartment, she is treated to traditional Jewish tales, including "Bavsi's Feast," "The Golden Shoes," "The Garden of Talking Flowers," and "A Phantom at the Wedding." See the 2003 reprint edition with new color illustrations by Anita Lobel.

Honor Books

Younger Readers

Judah Who Always Said "No" by Harriet Feder.
Illustrations by Katherine Janus Kahn.
Kar-Ben Publishing
ISBN: 0929371143

Brave Judah, a leader in the resistance to the changes a Greek king tries to force upon the Jews of Jerusalem, takes part in a stunning victory celebrated today as Hanukkah.

The World's Birthday: A Rosh Hashana Story by Barbara Diamond Goldin.
Illusrations by Jeanette Winter.
Harcourt Brace
ISBN: 0152000453

Daniel is determined to have a birthday party for the world to celebrate Rosh Hashanah.

Older Readers

Shadow of the Wall by Christa Laird.
Greenwillow Books
ISBN: 0688152910

Living with his mother and two sisters in the Warsaw Ghetto, Misha is befriended by the director of the orphanage, Dr. Korczak, and finds a purpose to his life when he joins a resistance organization.

The Cat Who Escaped from Steerage by Evelyn Wilde Mayerson.
Simon & Schuster
ISBN: 0684192098

As nine-year-old Chanah and her family journey from their native Poland to seek a new life in America, Chanah worries about the possible fates of her deaf-mute cousin Yaacov and of Pitsel, the cat she had rescued in Marseilles and smuggled aboard ship.

Notable Books

Younger Readers

Sophie's Name by Phyllis Grode.
Illustrations by Shelly O. Haas.
Kar-Ben Publishing
ISBN: 0929371186

Sophie Davida Finkle-Cohen thinks her name is too long and begs her family to call her "Sue," but as she learns about her namesakes, "Sue" begins to change her mind.

Fancy Aunt Jess by Amy Hest.
Illustrations by Amy Schwartz.
Morrow Junior Books
ISBN: 0688080960
Becky loves to spend weekends in Brooklyn with her ebullient, vibrant Aunt Jess and is delighted that she helps Aunt Jess find the perfect man at Shabbat services.

The Ring and the Window Seat by Amy Hest.
Illustrations by Deborah Haeffele.
Scholastic
ISBN: 0590413503

Although she has been saving for a ring, Stella gives her sock full of nickels to a Jewish carpenter who is trying to rescue his little girl from Nazi-controlled Europe.

Latkes and Applesauce by Fran Manushkin.
Illustrations by Robin Spowart.
Scholastic
ISBN: 0590422618

When a blizzard leaves a farm family housebound for Hanukkah, they share what little they have with some starving animals who later return the favor, allowing the family to celebrate with *latkes* and applesauce on the eighth night.

When Will the Fighting Stop?: A Child's View of Jerusalem by Ann Morris.
Photographs by Lilly Rivlin.
Atheneum
ISBN: 0689315082

A young Jewish boy living in Jerusalem observes all the different people living in the city and wonders why they can't all be friends.

The Little Old Man and His Dreams by Lillian Hammer Ross.
Illustrations by Deborah Healy.
Harper & Row
ISBN: 0060250941

God comes to an old man in his dreams and allow him to attend his granddaughter's wedding, but in return the old man must come to live with God. A sophisticated picture book for the older child.

Happy Passover, Rosie and Leo and Blossom's Sukkah by Jane Breskin Zalben.
Henry Holt
ISBN: 0805012214; 0805012265

Two charming small picture book holiday tales of a family of bears and their celebrations.

Older Readers

Lone Star by Barbara Barrie.
Delacorte Press, an imprint of Random House
ISBN: 0385301561

Actress Barrie's first book relates the story of a young Jewish girl forced to move with her family from their comfortable life in Chicago to Corpus Christi, Texas. As she adjusts to her new surroundings, her Orthodox grandfather is repelled by this assimilated lifestyle.

Menorahs, Mezuzas, and Other Jewish Symbols by Miriam Chaikin.
Illustrations by Erika Weihs.
Clarion Books
ISBN: 0899198562

Explains the history and significance of many Jewish symbols such as the Star of David, Menorah, *mezuza*, and holiday symbols and rituals.

The Answered Prayer and Other Yemenite Folktales by Sharlya Gold and Mishael Maswari Caspi.
Illustrations by Marjory Wunsch.
Jewish Publication Society
ISBN: 0827603541

Interesting rich folktale collection perfect for the storyteller or reader.

The House on Walenska Street by Charlotte Herman.
Illustrations by Susan Avishai.
Dutton
ISBN: 0525445196

An easy-to-read chapter book about eight-year-old Leah, her two younger sisters, and their widowed mother living in a small Russian *shtetl* in 1913.

Code Name Kris by Carol Matas.
Scribner's
ISBN: 068419208X

After the Nazi occupation of Denmark forces his Jewish friends to flee the country, 17-year-old Jesper continues his work with the underground resistance movement; sequel to *Lisa's War.*

Independence Avenue by Eileen Bluestone Sherman.
Jewish Publication Society
ISBN: 0827603673
Elias, a 14-year-old Russian immigrant, arrives alone in Kansas City in 1907, finding new employment and friends, but also receiving bad news about his family back in Russia.

A Tree Stands Still: Jewish Youth in Eastern Europe Today by Yale Strom.
Philomel Books
ISBN: 0399221549

A collection of interviews in which young people from Eastern Europe tell what life is like as a descendant of Holocaust survivors.

Hear O Israel: A Story of the Warsaw Ghetto by Terry Walton Treseder. Illustrations by Lloyd Bloom.
Atheneum
ISBN: 0689314566

A boy describes life in the Warsaw Ghetto and his family's ultimate transference to and decimation at Treblinka.

The Streets Are Paved with Gold by Fran Weissenberg.
Harbinger House
ISBN: 0943173515

14-year-old Debbie Gold and her school and family life in Brooklyn during the 1920's is the subject of this novel, the winner of the 1988 Sydney Taylor Manuscript Award.

1989 Awards

Younger Readers

Berchick by Esther Silverstein Blanc.
Illustrations by Tennessee Dixon
Volcano Press
ISBN: 0912078812

Homesteading in Wyoming in the early 1900's, a Jewish mother develops an unusual relationship with a colt she adopts named Berchick.

Older Readers

Number the Stars by Lois Lowry
Houghton Mifflin
ISBN: 0440227534

In 1943, during the German occupation of Denmark, ten-year-old Annemarie learns how to be brave and courageous when she helps shelter her Jewish friend from the Nazis.

Honor Books

Younger Readers

Grandma's Soup by Nancy Karkowsky
Illustrated by Shelly O. Haas.
Kar-Ben Publishing
ISBN: 0930494997

A young girl confronts her grandmother's growing confusion and disability from Alzheimer's disease.

Hershel and the Hanukkah Goblins by Eric Kimmel.
Illustrated by Trina Schart Hyman
Holiday House
ISBN: 0823411311

Relates how Hershel outwits the goblins that haunt the old synagogue and prevent the village people from celebrating Hanukkah.

The Old Synagogue by Richard Rosenblum.
Jewish Publication Society
ISBN: 0827603223

A once-beautiful synagogue on a crowded street in a big city is abandoned and becomes a factory when the original neighborhood inhabitants become more prosperous and move away; but as time goes by young Jewish families rediscover the area, move in, and restore to beauty the old synagogue.

Older Readers

***Pink Slippers, Bat Mitzvah Blues* by Ferida Wolf.**
Jewish Publication Society
ISBN: 0827605315

Thirteen-year-old Alyssa tries to balance the conflicting demands of ballet training with finding her place as a Jew in today's world.

***Silver Days* by Sonia Levitin**
Atheneum
ISBN: 0689715706

In this sequel to *Journey to America*, the reunited Platt family works hard at settling in to America, but the spectre of the war in Europe continues to affect their lives.

***Lisa's War* by Carol Matas.**
Scholastic
ISBN: 0590435175

During the Nazi occupation of Denmark, Lisa and other teenage Jews become involved in an underground resistance movement and eventually must flee for their lives.

Notable Books

Younger Readers

Malke's Secret Recipe: A Chanukah Story from Chelm by David A. Adler.
Illustrated by Joan Halpern.
Kar-Ben Publishing
ISBN: 0930494881

In the town of Chelm, Berel, the shoemaker, tries to duplicate Malke's recipe for latkes, but his wife's interference makes the plan go awry in a typically Chelm-like way in a tale illustrated with sprightly black and white drawings.

The Story of Hanukkah by Amy Ehrlich.
Illustrations by Ori Sherman.
Dial Books
ISBN: 0803706154

Noteworthy because of the magnificent illustrations by Ori Sherman, this story of Hanukkah is suitable for all ages. Also stunningly designed and illustrated by Sherman is *Four Questions* by Lynne Sharon Schwartz (Demco Media, 1994).

Not Yet, Elijah by Harriet Feder.
Illustrations by Joan Halpern.
Kar-Ben Publishing
ISBN: 0930494946

Mirroring the impatience of a child to get to his part in the Passover Seder, an increasingly agitated Elijah waits at the door until it is time for him to enter.

ABC: The Alef-Bet Book, the Israel Museum, Jerusalem by Florence Cassen Mayers.
Abrams
ISBN: 0810918854

This unique alef-bet book features breathtaking photographs of artifacts for each letter of the Hebrew alphabet. For all ages.

Mommy Never Went to Hebrew School by Mindy Avra Portnoy.
Illustrations by Shelly O. Haas.
Kar-Ben Publishing
ISBN: 0930494962

While looking at some old photographs, David, aged 8, discovers that his mother was not born a Jew and in this sensitive book learns the story of his mother's childhood, his parents' courtship, and her conversion.

***Minnie's Yom Kippur Birthday* by Marilyn Singer.**
Illustrations by Ruth Rosner.
Harper & Row
ISBN: 0060258462

When Minnie's fifth birthday falls on Yom Kippur, she wonders what the special events of the day will be as the ritual of the holiday unfolds.

Older Readers

***We Remember the Holocaust* by David A. Adler.**
Henry Holt
ISBN: 0805004343

First hand interviews with Holocaust survivors and numerous photographs help history come alive in this powerful account of Hitler's campaign against the Jews.

***Feathers in the Wind* by Miriam Chaikin.**
Illustrations by Denise Saldutti.
Harper & Row
ISBN: 0060211628

This latest story about Yossi, a young Yeshiva student, teaches that what is learned from the Torah is applicable to our lives today in this reworking of an old rabbinic tale.

***The Wailing Wall* by Leonard Everett Fisher.**
Macmillan
ISBN: 0027353109

Survey of the history of the Jewish people in Palestine and their activities around the First and Second Temples the site of which is now marked by the Western or Wailing Wall, with an emphasis on events before 70 A.D.is marked by Fisher's dramatic gray and white pictures of the Western Wall.

***Does God Have a Big Toe?* by Marc Gellman.**
Illustrations by Oscar de Mejo.
Harper Junior Books,
ISBN: 0060224320

Both lively and reverent, this collection of modern Midrashim about familiar Bible stories demonstrates the warm relationship between God and man.

Earth to Andrew O. Blechman by **Jane Breskin Zalben.**
Farrar Straus and Giroux
ISBN: 0374319162

When fourth grader Andrew agrees to tutor ex-vaudevillian Mr. Pearlstein in Hebrew, the stage is set for many jokes and the story of a well-depicted, close-knit family.

Teen Readers

Father of the Orphans: The Story of Janusz Korczak by **Mark Bernheim.**
Lodestar, an imprint of Dutton
ISBN: 0525672656

A moving biography of the assimilated Polish Jewish doctor and promoter of children's rights who chose death in Treblinka with his orphans over the freedom offered him.

The Other 1492: Jewish Settlement in the New World by **Norman Finkelstein.**
Scribner
ISBN: 0684189135

This competently researched book, illustrated with many reproductions of original documents, focuses on the expulsion in 1492 of the Jews from Spain.

The World of the Bible for Young Readers by **Yair Hoffman.**
Viking-Kestrel
ISBN: 0670817392

This colorful and approachable history of the Bible, both Jewish and Christian, is told from a Jewish historical perspective and is highlighted by more than 300 reproductions of documents, manuscripts and artifacts.

Plots and Players by **Pamela Melnikoff.**
Bedrick/Blackie
ISBN: 0872264068

Robin, Philip and Frances, young Jews in 16th century England, fight against the poison of prejudice while trying to save the life of Queen Elizabeth's Jewish doctor.

Beyond Safe Boundaries by Margaret Sacks.
Lodestar, an imprint of Dutton
ISBN: 0525672818

Jewish values abound in this novel of South Africa in the 1950s and 1960s in which Elizabeth becomes increasingly aware of the injustice in her society.

We Were Not Like Other People by Efraim Sevela.
Harper & Row
ISBN: 0060255072

Spanning six years and Russian terrain from Siberia to Germany, this is the story of a 12-year-old Jewish boy, separated from his Red Army parents by World War II and his survival against all odds.

1988 Awards

Younger Readers

The Keeping Quilt by Patricia Polacco.
Simon & Schuster
ISBN: 0689844476

A homemade quilt ties together the lives of four generations of an immigrant Jewish family, remaining a symbol of their enduring love and faith.

Older Readers

The Devil's Arithmetic by Jane Yolen.
Viking-Kestrel
ISBN: 0142401099

Hannah resents the traditions of her Jewish heritage until time travel places her in the middle of a small Jewish village in Nazi-occupied Poland.

Honor Books

Younger Readers

From Head to Toe: A Book about You by Yaffa Ganz.
Illustrations by Harvey Klineman.
Feldheim
ISBN: 0873064461

Describes the main parts of the human body, how they work, and how Jewish people employ all parts of their bodies in the service of God.

The Ark by Arthur Geisert.
Houghton Mifflin
ISBN: 0618006087

Retells the familiar Bible story, using etchings as illustrations, and vividly depicting life inside the ark.

Beni's First Chanukah by Jane Breskin Zalben.
Henry Holt
ISBN: 0805004793
On the first morning of Chanukah, Beni the bear eagerly prepares for the evening's festivities. Then he and his squirrel friends spend a wonderful evening filled with love and joy.

Older Readers

Out of Many Waters by Jacqueline Dembar Greene.
Walker
ISBN: 0802774016

Kidnapped from their parents during the Portuguese Inquisition and sent to work as slaves at a monastery in Brazil, two Jewish sisters attempt to make their way back to Europe to find their parents, but instead one becomes part of a group founding the first Jewish settlement in the United States.

David and Max by Gary and Gail Provost.
Jewish Publication Society
ISBN: 0827603924

When twelve-year-old David spends the summer with his grandfather Max, he helps him search for a friend who perished during the Holocaust., and learns about Max's life during World War II.

Teen Readers

Rescue: The Story of How Gentiles Saved Jews in the Holocaust by **Milton Meltzer.**
Harper and Row
ISBN: 0064461173

Detailing an often neglected side of the Holocaust, this study examines the courage and human decency of ordinary people who risked their lives to rescue Jews from Nazi extermination.

Notable Books

Younger Readers

Rachel and Mischa by **Steven and Ilene Bayer.**
Illustrations by Marlene L. Ruthen; Photographs by Joanne Strauss.
Kar-Ben Publishing
ISBN: 0930494776

This photo essay contrasts the lives of two Jewish children, one American and one Russian, and how they practice their religion.

And Shira Imagined by **Giora Carmi.**
Jewish Publication Society
ISBN: 082760288X

Dramatic pictures from young Shira's imagination interpret the actual places that Shira and her family visit in Israel.

The Donkey's Story: A Bible Story by **Barbara Cohen.**
Illustrations by Susan Jeanne Cohen.
Lothrop, Lee & Shepard
ISBN: 0688041043

This humorous retelling of the Bible tale in which the prophet Bilaam is asked to curse the Jewish people emphasizes the wise donkey's point of view.

Justin's Hebrew Name by **Ellie Gellman.**
Illustrations by Barbara Gellner.
Kar-Ben Publishing
ISBN: 0930494784

Justin begins Hebrew school without a Hebrew name. With the help of this classmates and an understanding rabbi, Justin acquires a name that is just right for him.

Just Enough Is Plenty: A Hanukkah Tale by **Barbara Diamond Goldin.**
Illustrations by Seymour Chwast.
Viking-Kestrel
ISBN: 0670818526

Although money is scarce this Hanukkah time, the generous family welcomes the mysterious peddler who leaves behind gifts and clues to this real identity.

Older Readers

A Kid's Catalog of Israel by **Chaya Burstein.**
Jewish Publication Society
ISBN: 0827602634

This mini-encyclopedia about Israel contains geography, history, stories, recipes, projects, songs, vocabulary and lots more.

The Mystery of the Coins by **Chaya Burstein.**
UAHC
ISBN: 0807403504

Two children and their grandmother discover some old coins which lead them through a study of Jewish history from ancient times to today.

Friends Forever by **Miriam Chaikin.**
Illustrations by Richard Egielski.
Harper & Row
ISBN: 0807403504

Set against the background of World War II, this latest in the stories of Molly and her friends, focuses on Molly's school experiences and her struggles to grow up.

Fire! The Library Is Burning by Barry Cytron.
Lerner Publications
ISBN: 0822505258

This well-organized book brings to life the disastrous fire and the rescue of thousands of books burned at the Jewish Theological Seminary in 1966.

And Then There Were Four by Miriam Elias.
Feldheim
ISBN: 0873064429
Four girls, all students at a Jewish day school, share laughter and tears, friendship and fears, as they become fast friends.

Anne Frank:: Life in Hiding by Johanna Hurwitz.
Illustrations by Vera Rosenberry.
Jewish Publication Society
ISBN: 0827603118

This is a simple, straightforward retelling of the Anne Frank story with a chronology and index.

Teen Readers

The Jewish American Heritage by David M. Brownstone.
Facts on File Publications
ISBN: 0816016283

A large number of period photographs and quotations enhance this basic overview of Jewish immigration to the United States.

Emma Lazarus by Diane Lefer.
Chelsea House
ISBN: 1555466648

In this clear, well-organized biography, both history and biography are entwined to give a complete picture of Emma Lazarus and her times.

Smoke and Ashes: The Story of the Holocaust by Barbara Rogasky.
Holiday House
ISBN: 0823406970

This well-organized, methodical and comprehensive study of the Holocaust is enhanced by numerous thoughtfully chosen photographs.

Touch Wood: A Girlhood in Occupied France by Renée Roth-Hano.
Four Winds, an imprint of Simon & Schuster
ISBN: 002777340X

This autobiographical novel tells the story of how a family of Jewish girls survives the war in Occupied France by being sheltered in a Catholic women's residence.

1987 Winners

Younger Readers

The Number on My Grandfather's Arm by David Adler.
Photographs by Rose Eichenbaum.
UAHC
ISBN: 0807403288
A little girl questions a number printed on her grandfather's arm and he explains how he received it in a Nazi concentration camp during World War II.

Older Readers

The Return by Sonia Levitin.
Atheneum
ISBN: 0449702804

Desta and the other members of her Falasha family, Jews suffering from discrimination in Ethiopia, finally flee the country and attempt the dangerous journey to Israel.

Notable Books

Younger Readers

Apple Pie and Onions by Judith Caseley.
Greenwillow Books
ISBN: 068806762X

A charming story of Rebecca and her Yiddish-speaking grandma, and the love and embarrassment she feels for her.

Even Higher by Barbara Cohen.
Illustrations by Anatoly Ivanov.
Lothrop, Lee & Shepard
ISBN: 0688064523

A favorite story by I.L. Peretz is ably retold with bright, colorful illustrations.

Gittel and the Bell by Roberta Goldshlag Cooks.
Illustrations by Susan Martz.
Kar-Ben Publishing
ISBN: 0930494687

Impish Gittel's desire to ring the village bell gets her into trouble with the elders of her *shtetl.*

Queen Esther by Tomie DePaola.
Harper & Row
ISBN: 0062555391

Beautifully and simply told with bright simple pictures by the noted author-illustrator.

My Sister's Wedding by Richard Rosenblum.
William Morrow
ISBN: 0688059554

Marrying a soldier -- what could be more exciting? The author's charming sketches draw the young reader into the simple story of his sister's wartime wedding in 1943.

Older Readers

Esther by Miriam Chaikin.
Illustrations by Vera Rosenberry.
Jewish Publication Society
ISBN: 0827602723

Retells the Old Testament story of how the young Jewish girl, Esther, became queen of Persia and used her influence to stop the evil minister Haman from killing all the Jews. The feast of Purim commemorates this event. A finely crafted book with delicate line drawings.

Exodus by Miriam Chaikin.
Illustrations by Charles Mikolaycak.
Holiday House
ISBN: 0823406075

Gloriously illustrated in full color with a poetic and complex text.

Yossi Tries to Help God by Miriam Chaikin.
Illustrations by Denise Saldutti.
Harper & Row
ISBN: 0060211970

Inspired by his rabbi's teaching that doing a good deed makes an angel, Yossi follows a plan that backfires and almost costs him his two best friends.

Joseph's Wardrobe by Paul J. Citrin.
Illustrations by Lindsey Aitken.
UAHC
ISBN: 0807403199

This collection of five *Midrashim*, set within a tale of marriage and intrigue in King Solomon's court, should appeal to those who love adventure stories.

The Christmas Revolution by Barbara Cohen.
Illustrations by Diane de Groat.
Lothrop, Lee & Shepard
ISBN: 0688068065

An excellent, enjoyable, and much-needed book in which all the "December issues" are raised.

First Fast by Barbara Cohen.
Illustrations by Martin Lemelman.
UAHC
ISBN: 0807403547

A meaningful story of ten-year-old Harry's first Yom Kippur fast.

Jerusalem, Shining Still by Karla Kuskin.
Woodcuts by David Frampton.
Harper & Row
ISBN: 0060235489

Appealing to adults and children, the handsome tinted woodcuts and serious poetic words outline the history of Jerusalem from the time of King David until today.

The Return of Morris Schumsky by Steven Schnur.
Illustrations by Victor Lazzaro.
UAHC
ISBN: 080740358X

Delightful irrepressible Morris Schumsky adds a few unexpected guests to his granddaughter's wedding and provides a meaningful twist to a special day.

Miracle Meals: Eight Nights of Food 'n Fun for Chanukah by Madeline Wikler and Judyth Groner.
Illustrations by Chari Rudin.
Kar-Ben Publishing
ISBN: 0930494717

Lots of fun and food in this new cookbook.

Teen Readers

Also Known as Sadzia! The Belly Dancer! by Merrill Joan Gerber.
Harper & Row
ISBN: 0060221623

Under pressure from her mother to lose weight in an exercise class, a sixteen-year-old Jewish girl rebels and joins a class in belly dancing where she finds independence, romance, and self-confidence--and an intriguing drummer named Sumir.

Eliezer Ben-Yehuda: The Father of Modern Hebrew by Malka Drucker.
(Jewish Biography Series)
Lodestar, an imprint of Dutton
ISBN: 0525671846

A biography of the Y, lost for 2000 years except for reading and writing, as an everyday language, thus uniting Jews of the modern world by providing a common tongue.

A Justice for All the People: Louis D. Brandeis by David Gross. (Jewish Biography Series)
Lodestar, an imprint of Dutton
ISBN: 0525671943

A biography of the lawyer, judge, popularizer of Zionist causes, and first Jew to serve on the Supreme Court, who helped end child labor in America, introduced the concepts of social security, minimum wage laws, and unemployment compensation, and, in short, devoted his life to social justice.

Daughter of My People: Henrietta Szold and Hadassah by Hazel Krantz.
(Jewish Biography Series)
Lodestar, an imprint of Dutton
ISBN: 0525672362

Traces the life of the Hadassah women's organization's first president, who dedicated its activities to improving the living conditions of Jews in Palestine.

The Book of Miracles: A Young Person's Guide to Jewish Spirituality by Lawrence Kushner.
Illustrations by Devis Grebu.
UAHC
ISBN: 0807403237

A carefully organized collection of *Midrashim*, retold and enhanced, with commentary by a leading theologian and masterful storyteller.

The Young Reader's Encyclopedia of Jewish History edited by Ilana Shamir.
Viking -Kestrel
ISBN: 0670817384

An attractive, ambitious volume filled with beautiful and informative color photographs and useful maps.

Forever My Jerusalem by Pu'ah Shteiner.
Feldheim
ISBN: 0873063945

This touching memoir of a young child's exile from Jerusalem and her triumphant return as an adult in 1967 has garnered much praise.

1986 Winners

Younger Readers

***Joseph Who Loved the Sabbath* by Marilyn Hirsh.**
Illustrations by Devis Grebu.
Viking Kestrel
ISBN: 0670811947

Despite his poverty, Joseph celebrated the seventh day with joy. A lovingly retold Talmudic tale, with finely detailed, full color drawings.

Older Readers

***Beyond the High White Wall* by Nancy Pitt.**
Charles Scribner's Sons
ISBN: 0684186632

Witnessing the murder of a peasant outside her small town in the Russian Ukraine in 1903, thirteen-year-old Libby triggers a wave of hate against her Jewish family, prompting them to consider immigrating to America.

Notable Books

Younger Readers

***Moses in the Bulrushes* by Warwick Hutton.**
Atheneum
ISBN: 0689503938

Retold in simple, dignified, unemotional language with exquisite pastel pictures.

***Ima on the Bima: My Mommy is a Rabbi* by Mindy Avra Portnoy.**
Illustrations by Steffi Karen Rubin.
Kar-Ben Publishing
ISBN: 0930494555

A simple story of daily life with Rebecca and her mother the rabbi.

The Big Sukkah by Peninnah Schram.
Illustrations by Jacqueline Kahane.
Kar-Ben Publishing
ISBN: 0930494563

Berel and his family have never had their many relatives to their small cottage to celebrate holidays, but one year at Sukkos, Berel has a brilliant idea for making a large space to entertain.

Yossel Zissel and the Wisdom of Chelm **by Amy Schwartz.**
Jewish Publication Society
ISBN: 0827602588
The littlest listeners will love the whimsical pictures and the obvious foolishness of Yossel Zissel while slightly older listeners and readers will laugh at the elaborate but increasingly worthless exchanges Yossel arranges for his gold.

Older Readers

Cooking the Israeli Way **by Jacqueline Bacon.**
Photographs by Robert L. and Diane Wolfe.
Lerner Publications
ISBN: 0822509121

A delightful and clear cookbook for children and parents.

Aviva's Piano **by Miriam Chaikin.**
Illustrations by Yossi Abulafia.
Clarion Books
ISBN: 0899193676

This little story, with its pleasant, whimsical drawings, includes plenty of illustrations, details and incidents to provide a feel of children's life at Kibbutz Kfar Giladi on the Lebanese border.

Sound the Shofar: The Story and Meaning of Rosh Hashanah and Yom Kippur **by Miriam Chaikin.**
Illustrations by Erika Weihs.
Clarion Books
ISBN: 0899193730

The final volume in Chaikin's holiday series discusses the origin and development of Rosh Hashanah and Yom Kippur, their major symbols, and ways of observing them in the world today and in different times in history.

A Torah Is Written by Paul Cowan.
Photographs by Rachel Cowan.
Jewish Publication Society
ISBN: 0827602707

A Beautifully written, beautifully photographed, beautifully designed book that communicates the love, spirit, care, and work that go into making a Torah scroll.

Poems for Jewish Holidays **edited by Myra Cohn Livingston.**
Illustrations by Lloyd Bloom.
Holiday House
ISBN: 0823406067

A small but delightful collection of poems with handsome substantial illustrations, this book will be enjoyed by children and parents together.

Hannah Szenes: A Song of Light **by Maxine Schur.**
Illustrations by Donna Ruff.
Jewish Publication Society
ISBN: 0827602510

A biography of the Jewish heroine whose mission to help rescue European Jews in World War II cost her her life.

The Narrowest Bar Mitzvah **by Steven Schnur.**
Illustrations by Victor Lazzaro.
UAHC
ISBN: 0807403164

This easy-to-read account of Alex's big day includes a broken water main that floods the Temple but Grandpa's narrow old house becomes the ark that brings Alex's *parsha*, the story of Noah, to completion.

The Great Jewish Quiz Book **by Barbara Spector.**
Jewish Publication Society
ISBN: 0827602596

A fun-filled, fact-filled quiz book that will entertain children and adults.

Teen Readers

***Uncle Jacob's Ghost Story* by Donn Kushner.**
Holt, Rinehart and Winston
ISBN: 003006502X.

A story filled with wonder, mysterious misdeeds, love, Polish-Jewish ghosts, and the Jewish immigrant experience.

***Sigmund Freud: Doctor of the Mind* by Marilyn Lager.**
Illustrations by Eric Lager.
Enslow Publishing
ISBN: 0894901176

A useful introduction to the life, studies and theories of Freud.

***I Lift My Lamp: Emma Lazarus and the Statue of Liberty* by Nancy Smiler Levinson. (Jewish Biography Series)**
Lodestar, an imprint of Dutton
ISBN: 525671803

A parallel story of the life of Emma Lazarus and the development of the statue.

***One Man's Valor: Leo Baeck and the Holocaust* by Anne E. Neimark. (Jewish Biography Series)**
Lodestar, an imprint of Dutton
ISBN: 0525671757

Includes the outline of Leo Baeck's life, actions, and philosophy with the focus on his heroic role in saving Jews during the Holocaust.

***Monday in Odessa* by Eileen Bluestone Sherman.**
Jewish Publication Society
ISBN: 0827602626

A story of a modern "refusenik" family.

The Floating Minyan of Pirate's Cove by Miriam Stark Zakon.
Illustrations by Sigmund Forst.
Judaica Press
ISBN: 0910818622

On the way to the solution of this fact-paced mystery, young readers will learn more about Jewish practice, events in the Bible, and modern Jewish history.

1985 Winners

Younger Readers

Brothers by Florence Freedman.
Illustrations by Robert Andrew Parker.
Harper & Row
ISBN: 0060218711

Hard times on adjoining farms bring about parallel acts of kindness and a celebration of "how good it is for brothers to live together in friendship."

Older Readers

Ike and Mama and the Seven Surprises by Carol Snyder.
Lothrop, Lee and Shepard
ISBN: 0688037321

Ike is very skeptical when his mother promises that he will have seven surprises in the month before his Bar Mitzvah, especially, with his father still hospitalized with tuberculosis and a newly-arrived, jobless cousin living in their small apartment.

Notable Books

Younger Readers

The Story of Mimmy and Simmy by Yaffa Ganz.
Illustrations by Harvey Klineman.
Feldheim
ISBN: 0873063856

Two girls are miserable being themselves until they trade places in a charming story that illustrates Pirke Avot 4:1.

The King in the Garden by Leon Garfield.
Illustrations by Michael Bragg.
Lothrop, Lee and Shepard
ISBN: 068804106X

A young girl helps the king in this account of Nebuchadnezzar's dreams and madness, magnificently illustrated by Michael Bragg.

I Love Passover by Marilyn Hirsh.
Holiday House
ISBN: 0823406962

Simplified retelling of the story and rituals of Passover, including the Seder. Bright, cheerful illustrations.

My First Book of Mitzvos by Ruth Schild Karlinsky.
Feldheim
ISBN: 0873063880

An Orthodox child performs mitzvoth throughout the day.

Watch the Stars Come Out by Riki Levinson.
Illustrations by Diane Goode.
Dutton
ISBN: 0525442057

Immigrant experience, not overtly Jewish but applicable. Wonderful pastel illustrations.

The Sign in Mendel's Window by Mildred Phillips.
Illustrations by Margot Zemach.
Macmillan
ISBN: 0027746003

A newcomer's evil intentions are foiled by Mendel's *shtetl* friends, in a tale enhanced by the Caldecott Medalist's evocative illustrations.

Who Will Lead the Kiddush? by Barbara Pomerantz.
Illustrations by Donna Ruff.
UAHC
ISBN: 0807403067

A young girl adjusts to the changes brought about by the divorce of her parents.

A Tree Full of Mitzvos by Dina Rosenfeld.
Illustrations by Yoel Kenny.
Merkoz L'Inyonei Chinuch
ISBN: 0826603637.

A tree tells young children about *mitzvos.*

The Very Best Place for a Penny by Dina Rosenfeld.
Illustrations by Leonid Pinchevsky and Eliyahu Meshchaninov.
Merkoz L'Inyonei Chinuch
ISBN: 0826603629

Wonderful introduction to the concept of *tzedakah*, with illustrations that are witty depictions of the text.

Washday on Noah's Ark by Glen Rounds.
Holiday House
ISBN: 0823405559

Delightful tall tale based on the biblical account, with humorous pastel illustrations.

Joshua's Dream by Sheila Segal.
Illustrations by Joel Iskowitz.
UAHC
ISBN: 0807404764

Joshua dreams of Israel, eventually planting his own tree there.

Older Readers

Ask another Question: The Story and Meaning of Passover by Miriam Chaikin.
Illustrations by Marvin Friedman.
Clarion Books
ISBN: 0899192815

Discusses the history and importance of Passover, a celebration of freedom commemorating the exodus of Moses and the Israelites from Egypt, where they had long been slaves, maintain the high quality of the holiday series.

Yossi Asks the Angels for Help by Miriam Chaikin.
Illustrations by Petra Mathers.
HarperCollins
ISBN: 0060211962

Yossi is back, asking the angels to help him retrieve the money he needs to buy Chanukah presents.

The Remembering Box by Eth Clifford.
Illustrations by Donna Diamond.
Houghton Mifflin
ISBN: 0395384761

Nine-year-old Joshua's weekly visits to his beloved grandmother on the Jewish Sabbath give him an understanding of love, family, and tradition, which helps him accept her death.

Secret Grove by Barbara Cohen.
Illustrations by Michael J. Deraney.
UAHC
ISBN: 0807403016

Beni and Ahmed reach an understanding beyond their elders. A wise, sad story about people, prejudice and political reality.

The Secret Spinner: Tales of Rav Gedalia by Howard Cushnir.
Illustrations by Katherine Kahn.
Kar-Ben Publishing
ISBN: 0930494474

Rav Gedalia gives modern lessons in ancient problems such as sharing and *tzedakah*.

Remember Not to Forget by Norman Finkelstein.
Illustrations by Lois and Lars Hokanson.
Franklin Watts
ISBN: 0531048926

The book presents the origins and history of anti-Semitism, beginning with the year 70 A.D., when the Jews were forced out of Jerusalem, to the founding of the State of Israel in 1948. Finkelstein uses specific incidents from history to illustrate how anti-Semitism stripped Jews of their rights and dignity. Dramatic woodcuts accompany Finkelstein's text.

***The Yanov Torah* by Erwin and Agnes Herman.**
Illustrations by Katherine Kahn.
Kar-Ben Publishing
ISBN: 0930494458

Story of the smuggling of a Torah into the Yanov Nazi Labor Camp, its rescue after liberation, and its journey to American in the care of a Soviet émigré.

***Rose Blanche* by Roberto Innocenti.**
Creative Education
ISBN: 1568461895

The magnificently illustrated story of a young German girl who experiences the Holocaust without understanding it.

***The Alef-Bet of Jewish Values: Code Words of Jewish Life* by Lenore C.**
Kipper and Howard I. Gogot.
Illustrations by Jana Paiss.
UAHC
ISBN: 0807402672

Letters of the Hebrew alphabet are used to teach about Jewish values and to present important Hebrew words. Examines twenty-three values of Jewish life using stories, Hebraic words, and scriptures from the Torah.

***Toba at the Hands of a Thief* by Michael Mark.**
Macmillan
ISBN: 0027623106

Presents eleven episodes from the life of a Polish teenager as she prepares to leave her Jewish family for a new life in America during the early 1900s.

***Shnook the Peddler* by Maxine Schur.**
Illustrations by Dale Redpath.
Dillon
ISBN: 0875182984

An unworldly peddler and a young boy with a guilty conscience are the heroes in a tale appropriate for Hanukkah reading.

***Before There Was a Before* by Arthur, David and Shoshana Waskow.**
Illustrations by Amnon Danziger.
Adama Books
ISBN: 0915361086

Thoughtful modern interpretation of the story of creation.

Teen Readers

***One Way to Ansonia* by Judie Angell.**
Bradbury Press
ISBN: 0027058603

Story of Rose's difficult life on the Lower East Side and of her escape.

***In Kindling Flame: The Story of Hannah Senesh, 1921-1944* by Linda Atkinson.**
Lothrop, Lee & Shepard
ISBN: 0688027148

Biography of Hannah Senesh with political and historical background.

***The Dream Keeper* by Margery Evemden.**
Lothrop, Lee & Shepard
ISBN: 068804638X

Both life in the shtetl and the problems of the contemporary Jewish family are part of this novel about 13-year-old Becka.

***Does Anyone Here Know the Way to Thirteen?* by Stephen Kaufman.**
Houghton Mifflin
ISBN: 0395359740

The story of too smart, too fat, Myron's Bar Mitzvah year.

***Star without a Sky* by Leonie Ossowski.**
Lerner Publishing
ISBN: 0822507714

A group of German young people must decide the fate of a Jewish boy that they find days before the Russians invade their town.

***Bar Mitzvah* by Sarah Silberstein Swartz.**
Doubleday
ISBN: 0385198264

An anthology for the Bar Mitzvah boy to browse in and return to again and again for further insights.

1984 Winners

Younger Readers

***Mrs. Moskowitz and the Sabbath Candlesticks* by Amy Schwartz.**
Jewish Publication Society
ISBN: 082760372X

Mrs. Moskowitz is unhappy in her new apartment until the discovery of her old Sabbath candlesticks prompts her into a series of activities that turn her new dwelling into a real home.

Older Readers
***The Island on Bird Street* by Uri Orlev.**
Houghton Mifflin
ISBN: 0395616239

During World War II a Jewish boy is left on his own for months in a ruined house in the Warsaw Ghetto, where he must learn all the tricks of survival under constantly life-threatening conditions.

1983 Winners

Younger Readers

***Bubby, Me, and Memories* by Barbara Pomerantz.**
UAHC Press
ISBN: 0807402532

Depicts the loss felt by a young child after the death of her grandmother.

Older Readers

***In the Mouth of the Wolf* by Rose Zar.**
Jewish Publication Society
ISBN: 0827603827

The author describes her experiences in wartime Poland and how she survived the Holocaust by passing herself off as an Aryan.

1982 Winners

Younger Readers

***The Castle on Hester Street* by Linda Heller.**
Jewish Publication Society
ISBN: 0827603231

Julie's grandmother deflates many of her husband's tall tales about their journey from Russia to America and their life on Hester Street.

Older Readers
***Call Me Ruth* by Marilyn Sachs.**
Bantam Doubleday Dell
ISBN: 0688137377

A young immigrant, newly arrived in Manhattan in 1908, has conflicting feelings about her mother's increasingly radical union involvement.

1981 Winners

Younger Readers

Yussel's Prayer by Barbara Cohen.
Illustrations by Michael J. Deraney.
Lothrop, Lee and Shepard
ISBN: 0688045812

A cowherd's simple but sincere Yom Kippur prayer is instrumental in ending the day's fast.

Older Readers

The Night Journey by Kathryn Lasky.
Penguin USA
ISBN: 0140320482

A young girl ignores her parents' wishes and persuades her great-grandmother to relate the story of her escape from czarist Russia.

1980 Winner

A Russian Farewell by Leonard Everett Fisher.
Four Winds Press
ISBN: 059007525X.

Depicts the anti-Semitic terror that finally drives Benjamin Shapiro, his wife, and 11 children out of Czarist Russia to America at the beginning of the 20th century.

1979 Winner

Ike and Mama and the Block Wedding by Carol Snyder.
Coward, McCann & Geoghegan
ISBN: 0698204611

Rosie Weinstein is getting married on Sunday but not without a little help from the residents of East 136th Street.

1978 Winner

***The Devil in Vienna* by Doris Orgel.**
Penguin USA
ISBN: 014032500X

A Jewish girl and the daughter of a Nazi have been best friends since they started school, but in 1938 the thirteen-year-olds find their close relationship difficult to maintain.

1977 Winner

***Exit from Home* by Anita Heyman.**
Random House
ISBN: 0517529033

A Jewish youth, training to become a rabbi in oppressive turn-of-the century Russia, becomes exposed to "worldly" ideas which change his attitude towards his religion and his country.

1976 Winner

***Never to Forget* by Milton Meltzer.**
Harper Collins Children's Books
ISBN: 0064461181

Describes Hitler's rise, the extermination of Europe's Jews, and the slow emergence of resistance, and includes first-hand accounts of ghetto life and death-camp terror.

1975 Winner

***Waiting for Mama* by Marietta Moskin.**
Coward, McCann & Geoghegan
ISBN: 0698203194

A Russian immigrant family living in New York in the early 1900's prepares for the long-awaited arrival of their mother and baby sister.

1974 Winner

No Award

1973 Winner

Uncle Misha's Partisans **by Yuri Suhl.**
Four Winds
ISBN: 0590072951

During World War II in the Ukraine, an orphaned Jewish boy joins a band of partisans who give him an important assignment against the Nazis.

1972 Winner

No Award (see Body-of Work Award)

1971 Winner

No Award (see Body-of Work Award)

1970 Winner

The Year **by Suzanne Lange.**
S.G. Phillips
ISBN: 0875991734.
Eighteen-year-old Ann Sanger leaves the Unites States, despite the opposition of her parents, with a group of young American and Canadians to help with the work of an Israeli kibbutz near the Syrian border.

1969 Winner

***Our Eddie* by Sulamith Ish-Kishor.**
Pantheon
ISBN: 039481455X.
Teenaged Eddie tries to make up to his family for his father's lack of warmth and
financial support, but seems doomed to tragedy at every turn.

1968 Winner

***The Endless Steppe* by Esther Hautzig.**
Harper Collins Children's Books
ISBN: 006440577X reissue paperback

The author describes her experiences during World War II when she and her family
were arrested by the Russians and sent to work in the Siberiangypsum mines.

Sydney Taylor Body-of-Work Award Winners

2018

Harold Grinspoon and PJ Library

PJ Library, a project of the Harold Grinspoon Foundation, is a family engagement program that sends free books celebrating Jewish values and culture to families with children aged six months through eight years old. This program has revolutionized the field of Jewish children's literature by providing dramatically improved access to Jewish books for families. It has also significantly increased the publication of children's books with Jewish content.

2004

Eric Kimmel

The author of over 50 children's books, Kimmel has written more than twenty books of Jewish interest during his illustrious career, including *Wonders and Miracles: A Passover Companion*, winner of the National Jewish Book Award and a 2004 Sydney Taylor Honor Book. He won the Sydney Taylor Book Award in 2000 for *Gershon's Monster* and in 1990 for *The Chanukah Guest*. Since garnering the award, Kimmel's *Hershel and the Hanukkah Goblins* (Holiday House, 1989) has become the best-selling Hanukkah book of all time, and several of his books have been named Sydney Taylor Notables, including *The Golem's Latkes* (Two Lions, 2011), which won the Jewish Book Council's Louis Posner Memorial Award for an Illustrated Children's Book.

2002

Judye Groner and Madeline Wikler

Founders of Kar-Ben Copies, these ladies published 8 Sydney Taylor Award and Honor Winners: *Sammy Spider's First Trip to Israel, Baby's Bris, The Magic of Kol Nidre, Shalom, Haver, Jeremy's Dreidel, Daddy's Chair, Judah Who Always Said "No"* and *Grandma's Soup*, as well as numerous other quality children's books with positive Jewish content. Kar-Ben was purchased by Lerner Publishing in 2001, and continues to publish books timely Jewish books.

1997

Barbara Diamond Goldin

Goldin is the author of 3 Sydney Taylor Award and Honor Winners: *Journeys with Elijah, Cakes and Miracles,* and *The World's Birthday,* as well as numerous other children's books with Jewish content like *Just Enough Is Plenty: A Hanukkah Tale* (1988), *The Magician's Visit* (1993), *Bat Mitzvah: A Jewish Girl's Coming of Age* (1995), *While the Candles Burn: Eight Stories for Hanukkah* (1996), *A Mountain of Blintzes* (2001), *One-Hundred-and-One Jewish Read-Aloud Stories: Ten-Minute Readings from the World's Best-Loved Jewish Literature* (2001), and *Night Lights: A Sukkot Story* (2002).

1989

Yaffa Ganz

Ganz is author of over 50 Jewish children's books depicting the lives of modern-Orthodox American children including the "Savta Simcha" series and the "Mimmy & Simmy" books. She served as editor for Feldheim's Rimon Series, and her timeless stories are being reissued for a new generation.

1984

Miriam Chaikin (1924-2015)

Chaikin was a long-time editor-in-chief of children's books in major New York houses. She published over 30 books for children of all ages including *A Nightmare in History the Holocaust 1933-1945* (1987), *Menorahs, Mezuzas and Other Jewish Symbols* (1990), *Clouds of Glory: Legends and Stories About Bible Times* (1997), *Angels Sweep the Desert Floor: Bible Legends About Moses in the Wilderness* (2002), and *Alexandra's Scroll* (2002).

1981

Barbara Cohen (1932-1992)

The author of the Sydney Taylor award winning book *Yussel's Prayer,* Cohen has also written over 20 children's books including *Thank You, Jackie Robinson* (1974), *Molly's Pilgrim* (1983), *The Secret Grove* (1985), *The Christmas Revolution* (1987), *Make a Wish, Molly* (1994), and *Here Come the Purim Players!* (1998).

1980

Sadie Rose Weilerstein (1894-1993)

Weilerstein is best known for her series of books about the adventures of a thumb-sized boy named K'tonton, published between 1935 and 1993. The *Best Jewish Books for Children and Teens* (Silver, 2011) notes that she played a "central role in the literary heritage of American Jewish children," and that the tradition of American stories for children about Jewish holidays had "come into their own" through Weilerstein's K'tonton books.

1979

Marilyn Hirsh (1944-1988)

Author of the Sydney Taylor award winning book *Joseph Who Loved the Sabbath*, also adapted and illustrated many traditional Jewish folktales: *Could Anything Be Worse?* (1974) *Captain Jiri and Rabbi Jacob* (1976), *The Rabbi and the Twenty-Nine Witches* (1977), and *Deborah the Dybbuk* (1978). Hirsh all illustrated several of Sadie Rose Weilerstein's K'tonton books.

1978

Sydney Taylor (1904-1978)

All-of-a-Kind Family, published by Follett in 1951, became the first commercially published, widely distributed children's book with a Jewish subject. She continued the adventures of the five Jewish sisters living in a 4 room apartment with their parents on New York's lower East Side in *All-of-a-Kind Family Downtown*, *More All-of-a-Kind Family*, *All-of-a-Kind Family Uptown*, and *Ella of All-of-a-Kind Family*. Sydney Taylor also wrote *A Papa like Everyone Else* and *Danny Loves a Holiday*.

1972

Molly Cone (1918-2016)

A life-long resident of Washington State, Cone authored 45 books for children of all ages published between 1960 and 1999 including picture books, biographies, and young adult fiction. Cone asserted that she wrote "about the way things are for ordinary kids—the ludicrous happenings in sometimes unhappy situations," with many stories based on her and her family's experiences.

1971

Isaac Bashevis Singer (1902-1991)

Polish-born American journalist, novelist, short-story writer, essayist, and recipient of the Nobel Prize for Literature in 1978, also wrote several books for children including *Why Noah Chose the Dove* (1973, illustrated by Eric Carle), *The Power of Light: Eight Stories for Hanukkah* (1980), *The Golem* (1982, illustrated by Uri Shulevitz), and several short story collections.

Index

Made in the USA
Las Vegas, NV
26 April 2025